"Theology at its best must equip pastors on
toring at its best will draw on the best of
shows us how all of that can happen. And
logian and a gifted hospital chaplain really
Together they impart much-needed wisdom... ... ... wonderful book."

—RICHARD MOUW
President emeritus, Fuller Theological Seminary

"This book is a gift. A work of profound pastoral and theological wisdom composed, not in the library, but at the hospital bedside. Here we find a hospital chaplain and a systematic theologian working together to make a fresh case for the deeper integration of pastoral care and Christian theology. Together they invite us to ask a rather uncomfortable but critically important question: What would happen to your theology at the bedside?"

—MATTHEW KAEMINGK
Fuller Theological Seminary

"Christian academics as well as ministers too often presume that 'doctrine' names an abstract discipline, one disconnected from the practical work of 'pastoral care.' This book displays the necessity—the inseparability—of theology for ministry. Far from rendering the minister a judgmental or distanced presence, these stories of chaplaincy illustrate how being tethered to the reality of the triune God frees us to love others in innovative, unexpected, and sometimes disruptive ways."

—ERIN DUFAULT-HUNTER
Fuller Theological Seminary

"This book aims at demonstrating the importance of the role of theology in chaplaincy and pastoral care. Its main title (*Good Tools Are Half the Job*) signals professional modesty as well as reflexive distance to its subject matter. Yet the fifteen pastoral presentations and theological meditations are most likely to move and illuminate their readers since they cover an immense span of what might be termed questions of life and death."

—MICHAEL WELKER
University of Heidelberg, Germany

"*Good Tools Are Half the Job* takes us on guided tours of the life and work of two theologians. One whose daily work traverses hospital hallways and requires standing alongside those undergoing illness, loss in various forms, and death. We get a front-row seat as Margriet offers the gift of accompaniment and spiritual and affective attunement to those facing the most painful experiences of life—and which is, from beginning to end, profoundly theological and relentlessly in pursuit of shalom. The other theologian has habitually transgressed the established pathways of academia for decades, running cross-grain to the narrow scholasticism that maintains its existence by keeping the suffering world at a safe distance. We look over the shoulder of Kees as he draws on ancient and modern voices to discern the subterranean roots producing the fruits of beauty and despair we regularly encounter. Wise and secure. Open to life's paradoxes and vulnerable to its brutal realities without crumbling, hiding, or anesthetizing. In *Good Tools Are Half the Job*, the van der Koois awaken us to wonder, awe, gratitude, and finally, to wisdom."

—CORY WILLSON
Calvin Theological Seminary

Good Tools Are Half the Job

Good Tools Are Half the Job

The Importance of Theology in Chaplaincy and Pastoral Care

MARGRIET & CORNELIS VAN DER KOOI

With a Foreword by Nicholas P. & Claire Wolterstorff

WIPF & STOCK · Eugene, Oregon

GOOD TOOLS ARE HALF THE JOB
The Importance of Theology in Chaplaincy and Pastoral Care

Wipf & Stock
An Imprint of Wipf and Stock Publishers
199 W. 8th Ave., Suite 3
Eugene, OR 97401

www.wipfandstock.com

PAPERBACK ISBN: 978-1-6667-1874-4
HARDCOVER ISBN: 978-1-6667-1875-1
EBOOK ISBN: 978-1-6667-1876-8

OCTOBER 18, 2021

Original title:
Gereedschap is het halve werk. De urgentie van theologie in pastoraat en zielzorg
2017, Uitgeverij Boekencentrum, Utrecht

Holy Bible, containing the Old and New Testaments with the Apocryphal/Deuterocanonical Books, New Revised Standard Version, New York/ Oxford, Oxford University Press, 1989.

Contents

Foreword

GOOD TOOLS ARE HALF THE JOB explores the intersection of pastoral counseling and theology on two levels. One of the authors is a chaplain; the other, a theologian. Each chapter opens with the chaplain describing a case in which she employed her biblical and theological wisdom in her engagement with a patient. The theologian then reflects on some of the theological issues that the case raises.

Hospitals are sites of anxiety and fear: fear by patients of permanent disability, of death, of what comes after death, of how their survivors will be cared for if they die. The anxiety and fear are often intertwined with disorientation. What the patient is undergoing makes no sense; it doesn't fit with how they have hitherto found meaning in their lives. They are suffering not only physically but psychologically and spiritually.

The chaplain listens attentively, often at length. She doesn't correct the patient, doesn't tell them that they shouldn't think, and shouldn't feel, the way they do. She listens. And as she listens, she reviews her knowledge of Scripture for a story, or her knowledge of theology for a theme, that will resonate with the patient, casting what they are undergoing in a new light, calming their anxiety and fear, restoring meaning, bringing some measure of spiritual healing. She doesn't instruct or direct. She suggests. In a couple of cases, she refers to stories by Tolkien and C. S. Lewis. Sometimes she highlights a piece of wisdom implicit, but unnoticed, in what the patient has said.

The psychological sensitivity evidenced in the cases described, and the amazing biblical and theological imagination, will be an inspiration for those seeking guidance in how to go about employing the resources of Scripture and theology in their practice of pastoral counseling.

The theological reflections evoked by the cases are as exemplary, in their own way, as are the cases. Occasionally the authors refer to theology as "dogmatics." But the theological reflections are not what most of us think of when we hear the word "dogmatics," namely, an abstract system of thought. Theology here begins from life—from life of a special sort, the engagement of a chaplain with a patient—and it consists of highlighting the theological significance of one or another aspect of the clinical engagement: highlighting the theological significance, for example, of glory, of hope, of the body, of God's universal revelation, of dreams, of forgiveness, of the Virgin Mary, of anointing the sick, and more, much more. Sometimes reflection on some aspect of the case leads the theologian to critique elements of traditional theology. Either way—whether theology illuminates the case or whether the case corrects theology—the theology in *Good Tools Are Half the Job* is always generous and gracious, never heavy-handed.

Pastoral counseling infused with theology, theology inspired by pastoral counseling: *Good Tools Are Half the Job* is a gift of insight and imagination to both chaplains and theologians, and to those of us who are neither.

Claire Wolterstorff, Episcopal priest and spiritual director
Nicholas Wolterstorff, Emeritus professor of philosophy, Yale University

Introduction

CHAPLAINCY, COACHING, PASTORAL VISITS, PASTORAL CARE: these are the terms we use for the help offered to people who are dealing with questions of life and death. The terms indicate the religious dimension at play—sometimes directly, more often indirectly—in people's life stories and search for direction and purpose. This book explores that religious and theological dimension through a series of case studies. Each starts with a concrete pastoral encounter, the story of a particular person and the way the chaplain reacts to their situation. We then reflect on these experiences from a theological perspective. How do theological convictions, notions, and emotions play a role—whether conscious or subconscious—in these encounters? More broadly, what are the connections between pastoral care and theology?

Our answers arise from the experience we have gathered over years of work in the chaplaincy and the university. From this we have come to a central, threefold conclusion. First, a solid theological basis is absolutely necessary for successful pastoral care. Second, theology is not an abstract system but a toolbox; good theology proves itself in practice. Third, pastoral care, talking with people, can be a source for renewed theological reflection. Our last chapter provides a more theoretical basis for this mutual relationship, and if the reader wishes, she can start with that. However, we think the best path into the subject is with Margriet's pastoral encounters. There we see theology at work, in the interplay between theology and the daily work of a chaplain.

The complexity of pastoral care is well captured in the painting of kite flyers on the cover of this book. Anyone who has ever tried kite-flying knows how important it is to have both good materials in the kite and the right kind of wind. Getting a kite aloft is an art in itself, and keeping it there demands constant concentration. A momentary lapse of attention, or pulling the string wrong, may cause a loss of control. The kite may crash to the ground and be damaged, or it may pull the kite-flyer along by its momentum. This is how it is with pastoral care, pastoral guidance, and coaching. Pastoral care is at least as much of an art as flying a kite. We hope this book helps you carry it out with effectiveness and grace.

Pentecost 2021, Margriet and Cornelis van der Kooi

Chapter 1

Mr. Çakir and the Salvation of the World

ONCE AGAIN MR. ÇAKIR has been admitted to our psychiatric ward. He is a Muslim, but he always attends church services when he is with us. Now besides that he wants a face-to-face meeting with me since—so he says—God, or rather Allah, has given him a special assignment. We set up a meeting which he starts by telling me about his vision and how it has been met with disbelief or indifference. "I have a big scar on my back from a serious car accident," Mr. Çakir explains. "The meaning of that scar has now been revealed to me." He gets up from his chair and declares with a solemn voice: "I am the reincarnation of Jesus Christ and of Mohammed, in one body. I have been told to save the world. I will bring peace to the entire world."

Then he looks at me very intently. "There is something else. Women with a name starting with the letter M are special. As, for instance, Maryam, whom you call Mary, the mother of Jesus. It has been revealed to me that, since your name starts with an M, you will have an important part in this divine work." He takes a deep breath: "You will be called the mother."[1]

I am neither a psychologist nor a psychiatrist. I know what people will say about Mr. Çakir, and they may be right. Psychotic. Megalomaniac. So it appears. But as a hospital chaplain I have a different role in this case. I need a different sort of diagnostic tool. Among other things, my toolkit has some good theology that helps me to listen closely to what Mr. Çakir is saying.

---

1. In his confused state Mr. Çakir thought both himself and a future son to be the Messiah.

This man is raising an important issue that I do not want to ignore: the desire for peace and justice, for wholeness, for a world without wounds. I hear the psychosis and megalomania in his words. But I would miss something important if these were the only things I noticed, or if I asked him whether he has taken his medication. There is something very healthy in what Mr. Çakir says: a sorrow that something has gone terribly wrong in the world, which needs to be healed.

I opened my toolkit and responded: "Mr. Çakir, I hear what you are saying. Thanks for sharing your thoughts with me and for your important insight that something must be done to heal and save the world. I fully agree with you. Just like you, I passionately long for peace and justice. And, like you, I do what I can to bring that about.

"Here is what I have to say with regard to your invitation to become the mother of the reincarnation of Jesus and Mohammed. In your tradition of Islam and mine in Christianity, we both believe that, if God calls me for a particular task, he will not only reveal this to you but also to me. So far he has not done so. But I promise you that I will try to listen closely to his voice when I read my Bible and pray.

"My second response is that I believe that the work you so passionately want to do has already been done by Jesus Christ. I also believe that God has promised that he himself will complete this work at the end of time. That is the good news. God is on your side when you say that the world must be recreated and renewed. I trust that God is on his way with this work. You and I can do what lies within our abilities, here and now, in the places where God has placed us. Nothing more and nothing less. You and I cannot bring the world to its final destination. God will bring peace and justice. I fully share that longing with you. Tomorrow I will give you a text that is almost two thousand years old about the coming of God's kingdom."

The next day I gave him a magnificent paraphrase of Revelation 21 written by a friend of ours, a great theologian, describing the new heavens and the new earth. I encouraged Mr. Çakir to cherish his desire and not to be distracted or discouraged by others—to hope and work and pray.

He accepted my gift and said, "You really think I can just leave this to God?"

I replied, "I truly believe that we must pray for the coming of God's kingdom."

"That is very important," he answered. As I was leaving he took my hand, laid it on his forehead, and then kissed it.

Walking away, I realized how grateful I am for the tools of my own profession. For the good news that God does not save us *from* the world but *with* the world. For his promise about the coming of justice and peace, about goodness, beauty, and truth.

This good news gave me a word for a vulnerable, psychotic person whose heart cherished a wholesome desire. It enabled me to do something different from the task of the doctors. Both tasks are needed but they are different things and must not be confused.

REFLECTION

Theology and multi-contextuality

Before we deal with the guiding role of the theology that we—consciously or subconsciously—carry with us, we need to say something about the present context of theological reflection as well as pastoral work. Where do we carry out these jobs? Just in church? Or should we broaden out beyond established religious institutions? To ask the question is to answer it. The context of theology has always been broader than the church. In this story it is carried out in a hospital—more precisely, in a closed ward at a psychiatric center. Here we find ourselves far outside the walls of the church, in a medical-care establishment. So in thinking about the importance and meaning of theology, especially of systematic theology, we must not only think of the church, sermons, or formal religious instruction. Systematic theology gets a startling new importance when we, once again, use it to look at the varied domains of real life.

Systematic theology, or dogmatics, is typically regarded as a discipline to be carried out in and about the church. And rightly so: the church and its proclamation are important points of reference. The term "dogmatics" stems from this relationship, for "dogma" first of all means those teachings that the church has determined to be the non-negotiable content of the Christian faith.[2] This determination came by way of a process of discovery that grew out of the church's early core confession regarding Jesus Christ, that "Jesus is Lord." This confession is the seed from which all Christian

2. By "theology" we mean reflection on the content and structure of the Christian faith. In Protestant seminaries "systematic theology" and "dogmatics" are common terms that are used interchangeably. We realize that "dogmatics," in particular, can carry negative associations. We hope to show that this view is not correct, that good dogmatics help and guide us in our everyday vocations.

dogma has grown. It is also a confession that sheds its light on all aspects of life—on "real life" in its full breadth and diversity. Thus theology and ethics must be linked to a whole range of social realities: our work and professions, sports, medical care, entertainment, and media old and new. Our society in its many dimensions and contexts thus comes into the theological spotlight and makes us come to grips with one the most important functions of dogmatics or systematic theology: to give us *orientation, direction*, and *purpose* for navigating the complexities of life.

We will return to this matter at this end of this chapter. But first let's turn to Margriet's conversation with Mr. Çakir.

The universality of the living God

In that conversation theological insights clearly exert a guiding influence. First, we notice that Mr. Çakir initiates the conversation. He is a Muslim, and he knows that the chaplain comes from a Christian background. This does not inhibit him from asking to talk; in his view the two religions have enough in common. Both honor Abraham, both assign a role to Jesus or Isa, and both have great respect for the woman Mary, or Maryam. This degree of openness on the part of a Muslim may seem strange to some Christians in light of the question of whether the God they worship is identical with Allah. Some answer this question with a strong "no": Allah is not the Father of Jesus Christ. What does it mean that Mr. Çakir is not troubled by this?

The actual conversation brings to the surface what the Christian faith and Islam have in common. Both religions worship a personal God, who can act. Both belong to the category of prophetic religions. The Reformed tradition in Christian theology has always offered a clear framework for understanding these and other striking similarities, even the degree of mutual recognition between the two religions. That framework is its doctrine of general revelation.[3] Of late this doctrine has received bad press in theological discussions and so has receded into the background. General revelation was rather easily identified with natural theology, that is, as an attempt to arrive at knowledge about God outside of God's revelation. But traditionally the doctrine of general revelation did not carry this connotation. General revelation was always taken to be the revelation of the living God, of the same God who revealed himself to Israel and in Jesus Christ. He, the living One, was precisely the One who also made himself known in

3. See Bavinck's classic, *Church between Temple and Mosque*.

his majesty and glory outside of the stream of salvation history. Therefore, it is better no longer to speak of general revelation but rather of the universality of God. More precisely, of how the working of God's Spirit touches people and makes them realize what they are missing: completeness, fulfillment. As one of my professors once put it: "God feeds his dearest children with hunger." That was the case with Mr. Çakir.

Theological tools

Hunger, longing—this is what Mr. Çakir feels amid all his misery: an overpowering, nerve-wracking hunger for a healed world. All the suffering in the world, the destroyed lives, the tragedies, the lack of fulfillment, the endless violations of persons and nature—it seems to spell chaos.

Mr. Çakir is the victim of chaos. He is being treated in the psychiatric ward because his own environment apparently could no longer cope with him. Perhaps he was a danger to himself and had lost touch with reality. The medical experts in this ward are sure of their diagnosis that he is suffering from psychoses. And that is what he is being treated for.

What can a chaplain do in such circumstances? She may be inclined to simply go along with the psychiatrist's assessment: this is a case of psychosis which has robbed the patient of his contact with reality, and his mental problems are expressing themselves through his delusions. Look at his grandiose "calling": the world is in trouble and he must play a crucial role in its salvation! The unique and perhaps also surprising element in the chaplain's interaction with Mr. Çakir is that she ignores the medical and psychiatric aspects of the situation. As a theologian she has her own instruments. She does not enter the field of psychiatric evaluation, but listens to Mr. Çakir's story with the ears of her own discipline, relying on what theology may offer her. Put another way, she does not join in the exclusive medicalization of the problem but taps some religious and theological resources.

We have gradually become accustomed to the medicalization of a great many of our problems. Dying, suffering, profound weariness, or even disgust with life itself (*taedium vitae*), a long string of mistakes and guilt—these are all problems that, if we are not careful, get only psychological or medical attention. Now certainly many problems in life do require medical or psychological care. Our society, however, runs the risk of immediately, and exclusively, reaching for pills, tranquillizers, antidepressants, and various other medications to even out our highs and lows. In the case of Mr.

Çakir the pastor instead focuses on what we could call the healthy part of the patient: his longing for a world that is "whole." From the perspectives of Judaism, Christianity, and Islam, this longing for a world made whole, for a heaven where God is all in all, is totally legitimate. Mr. Çakir's psychoses have some wholesome roots: longing and hope.

This pastoral encounter thus offers an interesting example of the theological perspective at work. Theology, or sound Christian teaching, tells us that people suffer because of a deep crevice in their existence, an absence of fulfillment, the limitations that hem us in due to the hard reality of evil. From this religious perspective, people have good reasons to long for salvation. This longing, and the pain that occurs when it remains unfulfilled, should not be dampened down or dismissed as lacking a sense of reality; it should be affirmed and endorsed. In this way the chaplain brings out an aspect of the situation that her theology has taught her: "Mr. Çakir, your longing is legitimate. It accords with a longing that is grounded in God, in Allah."

But the chaplain must do more. She must deal with the role Mr. Çakir in his delusions has assigned to her. The name Margriet begins with the same letter as Maryam, Miriam, and Mary. Mr. Çakir has picked up on this; he thinks he has hit upon a seam of gold. For him these female names offer a model for life, representing women who gave birth to a prophet and savior. Even in Mr. Çakir's psychosis we see an interesting meeting of Christianity and Islam. And in that joint scenario he is to play a crucial, messianic role!

Disclosures and revelations

Thus, the conversation touches not only on the themes of redemption and eschatology but also on a third subject in Christian theology: prophecy and revelations. The chaplain in this real-life story reacts to the revelations Mr. Çakir claims to have received in a way that differs significantly from what most mainstream textbooks on systematic theology tell us. That standard view barely considers the possibility of revelations and prophetic disclosures. For that we must go to Pentecostal or charismatic theology or to the circles of New Age religion. Modern academic theology, whether more liberal or more orthodox, is quite wary of revelations (in the plural). Over the last two centuries it has adhered, knowingly or not, to a view of revelation that became fashionable under the influence of nineteenth-century philosophic idealism. So it has become customary to say that the Bible is God's *self*-revelation.[4] All revelation is put under that heading. Certainly, from an eschatological perspective, that understanding is correct. But it is insufficient if we take salvation history seriously. The Bible refers to *revelations*, in the plural. The content of Peter's vision in Acts 10:9–15, which instructs him to revise his attitude toward unclean food, or of the vision of Paul in Acts 16:9, in which he is told to cross over into Europe, is not God. The content in these and other biblical revelations concerns a task; it conveys a message, not God's self-revelation.

In any case, the chaplain does not try to deny the reality or doubt the possibility that Mr. Çakir has received a prophetic message. Her reply assumes that we might well receive such. Her question, rather, goes to the matter of how the receiver of the message is involved in the experience. In other words: she implicitly introduces the matter of "discerning the spirits" by bringing up the crucial criterion: how do we identify the source of the message that Mr. Çakir reports to her?

Here she places both herself and Mr. Çakir under God's authority: "This is my answer to your invitation to become the mother of the reincarnation of Jesus and Mohammed. On the basis of your Islamic tradition and mine in Christianity we both believe that, if God has assigned me a task, he will not only inform you but also me. To date he has not done so, but I promise you that I will listen carefully to his voice when I read my Bible and pray." This answer accords with a possibility that is found in both the biblical tradition and in Islam. But in one and the same breath it also makes a correction, or rather, gives the steering wheel a corrective pull. The chaplain both connects with the known and offers a rectification. The person for whom the message is intended must receive that message herself. The prominent examples of such a message or announcement are, of course, the annunciations to Zachariah and to Mary. This move places both partners in the conversation—Mr. Çakir as well as the chaplain—within the sphere of God's active presence. Both may be addressed with a message from God. Note that this method of simultaneously connecting and correcting does not for a moment create a sense that Mr. Çakir is not taken seriously. On the contrary, both parties share a common ground which is defined by a story of God and God's people. This story presupposes that God speaks, can be spoken to, and acts concretely; further, that God, as the acting subject, wants to reach a goal, namely the creation of a perfect world.

4. For a fuller discussion, see Van der Kooi, *As in a Mirror*, 229–315.

Messianism

When she brings up this perfect world, we see the chaplain offering another correction concerning the messianic role Mr. Çakir claims for himself. She reminds him of the place of Jesus in the story: "I believe that the work you so fervently want to do has already been done by Jesus Christ." This touches on an essential difference between Christianity and Islam, on the question of how human beings and the world are to be saved. The Christian doctrine of salvation speaks in terms of something that has been completed, and so, at the chaplain's hands, it "overrides" the messianic task that Mr. Çakir claims for himself. Introducing a decisive element of Christian soteriology into the conversation, the chaplain reconstructs the picture sketched by Mr. Çakir. His story is that he himself is predestined to save the world as the reincarnation of Christ and Mohammed. Her answer is that he is no longer needed, that he is too late—Christ has already done this. But further, that wherever we are, we can and must live in expectation of this new world. This by no means implies a passive attitude. In other words, the chaplain has placed the experience of Mr. Çakir within the horizon of Christian theology and has pointed him in a direction that, at the same time, supplies a correction. Theology most definitely has this guiding role.

Orientation

Let's return to the matter we discussed at the start of this reflection—of the various ways in which theological concepts, sometimes consciously but more often unconsciously, contribute to the work of pastoral care. The title of this book describes theology in terms of a toolkit. A toolkit contains different instruments for different tasks. The first task that theology takes up in pastoral care is to provide *orientation*. In the story of Mr. Çakir the chaplain does just that by finding ways, among the various possibilities at hand, to keep the conversation going while steering it in a particular direction. She has to work with Mr. Çakir's account and his longing for a world of wholeness, justice, and peace. A second important function of doctrine becomes visible here: the *corrective* or *normative* function. At the same time, the third, *descriptive* function of dogmatics—that is, sorting out the meaning of faith and the relationships among the various parts of the theological system—hardly plays any role in this particular case. In our time it makes sense to emphasize this first function of dogmatics, of giving *orientation*. Yet, considering the enormous varieties on offer in the marketplace of religion and worldviews, it is also important to pursue the third function and explain the meaning of the Christian faith. To use an older characterization: dogmatics is not primarily a theoretical but above all a practical discipline. It focuses on salvation and our life in this world, and in the world to come.

Chapter 2

Stones for Bread
A Controversy about Salvation

Since I work as a chaplain on behalf of a church, and since I consider this link with the church to be essential, I asked my regional denominational board for an opportunity to speak to them about my work and answer any questions they might have.

I had no sooner started my talk than I heard myself remarking that I find my work becoming increasingly heavy. Not because I am confronted with sickness, sadness, and death. These are tough challenges, certainly, but they come with the job. Neither is it because of secularization in society, for this has been with me for a long time. No, what I find more and more taxing, even shocking, is secularization within the institution that has called me to this work: the church. We live in a world in which the people almost completely focus on themselves. Everything is about personal growth and freedom, about authentic meaning (whatever that might be). Spirituality (whatever *that* is) is a self-made product, with an ironclad doctrine that it *is* good when it *feels* good. Not to be critical, but this is not enough for me. The light must stream from the Outside to the inside, as I myself do not generate enough light. Meaning must be given, not exacted, made, arranged, or diluted according to our own ideas. Otherwise, it will neither satisfy me nor enable me to support others.

DEALING WITH DEATH

A father was telling me about the funeral of his young son. At his wife's urging it was led by a female funeral director who was "spiritual but not religious." Both parents had once been active in church youth work, the father had been a long-time member of the local church board, but their relationship with the local church had gradually deteriorated. At the end of the ceremony a blue butterfly had descended on the small coffin before it was put in the ground. The funeral director had commented, "Look, your little boy wants to tell you that everything is okay." She had looked around her with a cheerful encouraging smile on her face. "This was all part of the package," the father fulminated later.

Those who were there had nodded emotionally. "How sweet," an aunt with a firm Reformed background had even whispered, "That will keep me going."

I almost exploded inside. Everything okay!? Sweet!? What nonsense! I can only call this giving stones for bread.[1] I remain silent for a moment and let the father speak. With barely contained anger he says: "At that moment I was robbed of my grief. Everything was okay. What do you mean, okay? Our little boy dead in a coffin, is that okay? For weeks I have been crying in despair. My wife does not agree with me. She thought it was beautiful. And whenever a butterfly appears, all questions are suppressed. Hurrah, here is our son once again dropping down from heaven. She cannot let him go. And I cannot find any comfort. I am afraid our marriage will not survive."

Stones for bread. Why is it that people give so much credence to this kind of talk? To such self-manufactured ideas? They provide just as little help as the harsh words we often hear in super-religious circles. They betray the same kind of delusion: the spiritual counselors (strangely enough, more often women than men) have accessed God's control room and are taking charge. They suggest they know how things really are. They claim a kind of authority for themselves. They invent their own rituals. They manufacture meaning which they anchor in nothing more than that it "feels good." I call this stones for bread because I cannot regard it as innocent. The mother in the story suspends her grief; she is comforted by butterflies and is cheated by the message concocted by her self-proclaimed guru.

And there was evening and there was morning, a new day. The father and I had agreed to meet in the quiet room of the hospital. I said, "I will

1. A saying of Jesus recorded in Matthew 7:9 and Luke 11:11.

tell you a different story. It is a story that is very meaningful to me as I hear all sorts of terrible things from working in a hospital. It may be meaningful for you too. You are in good company with all your anger and grief. In his Gospel John relates a story that, I think, does justice to grief (John 11). It is about a friend of Jesus, Lazarus, who died. He must have been about the same age as Jesus, about thirty, I think. Too young to die. Jesus is called, but when he arrives at the village, his friend is already dead and buried. The story has an unbelievable ending, but it comforts me a lot to see that Jesus is angry and that he grieves when he arrives at Lazarus's tomb. He is angry and he grieves! Apparently, there is something about death that makes it impossible for us to see it as dear or acceptable. The story tells us that Jesus is in tears. The form of the verb that is used does not refer to a soft sobbing but to loud, intense weeping. And there is also anger! Some Bible versions have opted for a translation that says that Jesus was irritated or disturbed, but that is far too superficial in view of the original word in the Greek text. He was angry with a kind of holy anger. You will understand that, certainly."

The father of the child who had died stared at an icon of the mother of God hanging in the room. She bears her son in her arms; she has a mournful look on her face, as if she already knows of her future suffering. The child presses itself against the mother. I hear a sigh, "This mother, the way she looks. I knew the story but had lost that knowledge. This is infinitely better; this is about acknowledgment." That was all that needed to be said.

I thought of another conversation that touched on the question of meaning. An elderly woman had been admitted and was now being transferred to our hospice, a good and loving place. Early on the morning of her transfer a young nurse invited her to go with her to the other side of our ward; she had brought a wheelchair with her. "Today's sunrise is beautiful, let's just have a look."

Later that day the lady said to me, "I have no idea whether that nurse is a believer, but she provided new hope. I don't know how, but it is as if I have regained my trust in God that he is still in charge."

"That hope has valid papers," I replied. Together we read the text from the ancient book of Lamentations: "Because of the Lord's great love we are not consumed, for his compassions never fail. They are new every morning; great is your faithfulness" (Lam 3:22–23).

There is nothing wrong with having a good feeling but let's not pamper ourselves too much. The church must find its anchor in the word of God, which is strong enough to keep us as we live and as we die, in body and soul. But all this is self-manufactured meaning: when push comes to shove it fails to give support.

REFLECTION

Collision

In both of these encounters we are dealing with "feeling good." But how do we evaluate that? The two episodes confront us with the question about the instruments theology gives us to determine whether this good feeling, this agreeable sense of wellness, is justified. Or, to use theological language: we are faced with the challenge of "discerning the spirits." The presence of the butterfly on the coffin of the dead boy prompted the spiritual funeral director to say, "Look, your boy wants to tell you that everything is okay." With these words she (perhaps subconsciously) made use of an image from Greek mythology. The Greek word *psyche* can be translated as "soul" but also as "butterfly," a caterpillar that emerges from its chrysalis and goes from one flower to the next, dancing in the light. Just so, the butterfly on the coffin is a signal from the boy who gives a sign of life from a different dimension. This interpretation fits with a New Age way of thinking derived from ancient mystery religion. When we die, it says, we start on a journey, are liberated, pass through other dimensions, but still remain who we are. Some are open to this approach and think it is beautiful. It might even seem to line up with the Christian teaching that those who have died are with God and enjoy some form of life in his presence. This opens up the old discussion of an interim period, or soul-sleep, between death and the resurrection.

The father of the dead child represents another reaction, the voice of pure grief that demands to be acknowledged. He protests loudly, totally disagreeing with the funeral director and his own wife. His son lies in the coffin, dead. A young life has been destroyed by sickness, broken in the bud. The spiritual lady to him does nothing but obscure reality, papering over a gaping hole. In addition, he is losing his wife in the process. She clings to the spiritual funeral director as her authority. Or rather: she *invests* her with authority and gains access to some esoteric wisdom. The father does not share in this experience. And, out of her Christian frame of reference, the chaplain openly agrees with him. She suggests another framework that contrasts with this New Age sense of peace. She demands room for pain, anger, despair, and anguish. She sides with the father, who, in passing, tells her that this totally different approach of the funeral director has caused a menacing rift in their marriage: "How will our marriage survive?" This happens rather often: a great tragedy and the different ways of coping with grief cause the end of many marriages.

The steering role of a fundamental theological framework is clearly visible in this story. What insight do we as human beings have with respect to divine government? Are chaplains, theologians, and spiritual counselors present with God in his control room? The response of the Christian chaplain is a resounding "no." Her choice of words supports the cry of anger, lament, and protest. She characterizes the theology of the spiritual funeral director as assuming control of the steering wheel with a self-manufactured faith. The chaplain is lashing out against a freewheeling spirituality that introduces its own doctrines, for it is typical for this kind of spirituality to select different elements from different religions and traditions and mix them into a new combination, a do-it-yourself patchwork or "bricolage." One problem in this scenario is its lack of quality control by any supervising authority that gives a mandate and assigns and regulates responsibilities. The response of the chaplain to this form of spirituality has a moral and political dimension, for she has seen that freewheeling spiritual counselors can pose a threat to mental health. In any case, the remarks of the spiritual counselor in this story are not innocent or neutral. They deny the realities of evil and loss and present things as more beautiful than they are. There is always a butterfly dancing on a grave.

The theology of the chaplain points in a different direction. She makes no appeal to the will of God nor suggests that God takes care of everything. The chaplain pushes answers to the why-questions some distance away and does so for reasons of sound pastoral theology: we are humans, on earth; we are not God and do not sit in his control room where we can check everything. We must hold a finger to our lips.[2]

The link with the overarching story

But what about the second episode: the woman in the wheelchair who is taken by a nurse to a window where she can watch a beautiful sunrise? Is there a theological justification for "feeling good" when seeing a colorful sky? "As if God is still in control," she says. The chaplain cites a well-known

2. See Job 38–39.

text from Lamentations 3, in which praise is offered to God at the break of a new day. The new day is a token of his care for us. Influenced by a one-sided reading of Karl Barth's theology, any reference to God's work in nature has sometimes been rendered suspect as "natural theology," an attempt to acquire knowledge of God apart from the revelation in Jesus Christ.

Fortunately, lately—even with all the ambiguity we discern in creation—more room has opened up for a theology of nature: a Christian theology in which admiration for the greatness of nature may be appreciated and interpreted within a Trinitarian context, in which the Father of Jesus Christ is acknowledged as the creator of this world. In other words: natural reality does not come from some unknown source but from God, the source of all that is good. Such a proposition is far from self-evident. In the second century we meet a certain Marcion, originally from Pontus on the Black Sea and around 140 CE a member of the church in Rome. The German theologian Franz Overbeck said that Marcion was the only person to really understand Paul, but that, at the same time, he also misunderstood the apostle. That is to say: Marcion understood that God's love has its center in the person and mission of Jesus Christ. Marcion interpreted this so consistently that he regarded Paul as the only real disciple of Jesus; for that reason, the Old Testament and major parts of the New Testament had no meaning for him. The Father of Jesus Christ, he felt, could not have been the creator because creation is too arbitrary, too cruel. Marcion therefore posed a hard separation between creation and redemption.

The Christian church did not agree with Marcion's proposal, however attractive it was for many in that culture. Neither did it support mystery religions that regarded evil and misery as mere appearances to be embraced as part of a fundamentally harmonious reality. The church kept the Old and New Testament together and placed creation and redemption alongside each other. This doctrinal decision went against the dominant perception of life at the time, and it violates yearnings we might harbor for a beautiful, smooth theology, for it leaves us with the question of how this loving God can also be the creator. The chaplain is aware of this. She leaves space for not-knowing, for bewilderment and bitterness in the face of loss, for lament and protest. But, at the same time, from an affective and theological perspective, this move opens up room for gratitude, for wonder, for a vote of trust that awaits a further unfolding. Christian theology, with its story of God as creator, redeemer, and renewer, thus provides us with the instruments to throw light on our experiences and to connect them with that overarching story. The experience of a rising sun can become a sign that God has not left his world to itself. It may even give us a glimpse of the work of the Spirit, since this Spirit already connects us in our present life with the future. These encounters perhaps provide us not so much with theoretical explanations or cohesive philosophies as help us see ways to accept and endure this life with all its cruelty and beauty. Good theology is prepared to accept gaps in our knowledge.

Chapter 3

The Child Who Steps Up
On Evil and Transformation

THE MAN FACING ME was angry. "My daughter's ex! For years I pampered that guy. We welcomed him as a prince, as a son! I gave him a job in my business. I taught him everything about Jesus, about sin and guilt and forgiveness; he was active in our local church and came to Bible studies. He said he was truly converted. And now he has left my daughter. He says he doesn't want to be my project any more. He says he has lost his identity. He wants to start his own life. What's this guy talking about? He owes me everything! Ungrateful dog! He better never knock at our door again! I don't ever want to see him again, and I have told him so very clearly. He should get lost. He will never again set foot in our house!"

I have a story that might give him some help but cannot share it with him right now. He is so angry that he would not hear what I say. I remain silent.

ANNA, PART I

I meet Anna in the quiet room of our hospital. She didn't get much of a Christian worldview growing up: at Christmas the family went to midnight mass, but what she best remembers is the meal that followed. Over the years as I got to know her, she told me her indescribably terrible life story, of one abuse following another. Uncles, cousins, a teacher, her ex: all seemed to sense that she was a vulnerable prey that they could do with as they pleased. Four years ago her son René, with slamming doors, anger, and reproach, broke all contact with her. "I am totally fed up," he had shouted on his way out. "I want nothing to do with my childhood."

It is written that evil and misery are transmitted to the third and fourth generation (Exod 34:7). As a young minister I found it very difficult to read those words from the pulpit. It sounded so unfair, as if people who had their own difficulties were being punished in addition for things that not they but their forebears had done. Then I saw that the problem reflects a law of psychology. One of our psychiatrists said: "Only when a strong child steps up to break the chain of familial violence, incest, addiction, criminality, and other miseries can something new be started."

"That Person has actually come," I said, "a Carpenter who I believe can make the key. But that does not mean that all problems are instantly solved."

Anna tells me she had a peculiar dream. "Over the years I have repeatedly told myself that if one day René would stand at my door, he would have a lot of explaining to do. If he showed up we would first need to have a serious discussion. But then I had this dream: René did come to the door and I was simply joyful, I only felt gladness. I embraced him. I had no questions. I did not tell him that we first had to talk. I was just happy and could not stop kissing him. And when I awoke, I continued to feel that joy and thought, it's going to be okay. Isn't that strange? And also, this dream gives me such confidence! Extraordinary! Do you find it strange?"

"It makes me think of an old story," I said.[1] "I am going to tell it to you for it is just as beautiful as your dream. It is a story from the Bible, told by Jesus. It is about a father who had two sons. The younger son wanted to do his own thing and was tired of being at home. I don't know why, that's not in the story. He demanded his share of the inheritance, as if it were already due to him. In fact, the younger son was saying that he just couldn't wait till his father was dead. He was only interested in his father's money. Very painful, I think. One could say that the son 'unfathers' his father.

"The story does not tell us whether the father feels terribly hurt; it only says that he remains at his post and is on the lookout to see whether at any moment his son will return. And so it happens. One day the son runs out of money and gets beaten at his own game: his so-called friends are only interested in his money and turn their backs on him. He learns what it is to

---

1. Luke 15.

be poor and hungry, and he decides to go back to where he came from. Not as the son, he realizes, for this is not possible. Maybe his father will employ him as a servant.

"I imagine he returned with a heavy heart. How will he be received? Will he be allowed to enter his father's house? Will the father read him the riot act? The story is delightful: the father has not given up on their relationship. Seeing his son coming from afar, he does not passively wait at the front door. We are told that he runs outside, throws himself on his son, and kisses him passionately. The boy does not even get the chance to say 'I am so sorry.' The father is simply overjoyed that his son is back."

Anna has listened attentively. I can see that she understands the story. I say, "In your dream you are like the father, and you're so happy when re-telling it. You embrace your son. You cannot and will not do anything else, no accusations. You are his mother and this, and nothing else, is what you want to do. It seems like God is telling you how you could react if René would suddenly appear at your door."

She was open to the story. "You won't let yourself be unmothered," I say. She looks so relaxed when she laughs. And that is what she now does.

ANNA, PART II

Many months and conversations later I unexpectedly received an e-mail from Anna: "Something in me made me ask whether I could forgive the men who abused me. It just popped up in my mind. Maybe you'll find it wrong, but I have concluded that this is really impossible for me. I cannot give them a license for what they did. And, if you don't mind me saying so: I hate these people."

I realized that some things can be more easily expressed by letter or e-mail. I wrote, "There needs to be some acknowledgment on the part of those who did this to you, that they did something evil, that they feel remorse and ask for your forgiveness. It's too much to ask to forgive the other party without any acknowledgment of what you have suffered. The only person who was truly able to do so was Jesus. Maybe you can decide to pray: 'God, this is simply beyond me. Here you have these men. I need to turn my back on them, I will no longer bother with them. I leave that to you.'"

Anna promptly responded: "You write that I could perhaps pray. But that is pretty difficult. You may not like to hear this, but I haven't prayed for a long time. Because God let me down. There, I've said it. I often felt abandoned when I called on him at moments when I was abused or mistreated and felt that I needed him so terribly. But nothing ever happened and the abuse and all the misery continued.

"I have to cry as I write these words, but I want to be honest with you. At the time I did not understand at all; I just felt let down and very lonely. I have to think deeply about this. I get what you say, but there still is this barrier. I am sorry to say this."

I replied, "Thanks for your e-mail and for trusting me. Let me, once more, be very clear: I am not disappointed about you not being able to pray, and I don't want to push you in any way. You do not have to fulfill any conditions, and this is not about making you into a super-believer—you cannot do so yourself and I even less. Plus I have no idea what such a super-believer would look like. The only thing that counts in our conversations is that you find a way out, that I listen and try to give you a handle on some things, and that we see whether or not that works. If it does, we will gladly explore things further; if it does not, we will set it aside. The fact that you cannot pray and feel that you were abandoned by people and by God is not strange. I find it very understandable.

"It surprised me that you introduced the term 'forgiveness.' We've never talked about this before. That was impossible, since what emerged in our talks was so big and so terrible. I have no idea what topics you may want to talk about in the future, but it seems to me that it is still premature to give forgiveness too much attention. What happened is simply too horrible. I think (and I have some valid papers, I mean old texts, to back me up) that you will find God on your side. I believe he is 'angry' (and this reminds me of the concept of 'holy wrath,' which goes much deeper than being angry or feeling regret) over what has been done to you. Perhaps you can find support from now having some good people around you, as you yourself have repeatedly said. Perhaps this is how God tells you that he has not abandoned you. An army of 'angels' has assembled around you. And what other way is there to describe angels than as messengers of God who show care and love?

"Just leave this theme for now; praying is not a 'must.' Others will pray for you, as I do, for instance. I wanted to give you some tools to remove this burden from your heart. 'Here they are, God, these men and their abuses; for now I am unable to deal with them, so, please, do this on my behalf.'

"I am convinced that for the time being this is enough."

REFLECTION

Dreams

Dreams, we are told, are not real. This encounter, however, shows that this is not always the case. At least not for someone who has some theological background and has, as a chaplain, more in her backpack than a dose of popular psychology. Indeed, René is not at the door. Anna *dreams* that her son has come home. Even though she had determined that, whenever he might ring the doorbell, she would not let him in until she had given him a piece of her mind, she hits upon another layer in her dream: the layer of her motherhood in which she is overpowered by another, more profound reaction. When he stands before her in her dream in a state of desperation, she can only be glad and kiss him passionately. The chaplain connects this reaction with a well-known Bible story: the story of the lost ("prodigal") son, or rather, of the expecting and welcoming Father. For the original hearers, who lived in a culture of shame, it must have been a scandalous story. It simply was not done—as it isn't now—to demand one's share of the inheritance while the father is still alive. The chaplain talks of the loss of his status as son. But the father remains the father and then one day sees his son coming down the road. He forgets any feeling of hurt and runs towards him. The Greek text conveys the idea of literal running. God on a run! Jesus uses this story to confront his critics, the religious and moral leaders of his day. The God of Israel cannot forget his children, not even those children who have gone astray.

Love is a strange thing. Anna's experience is pulled into this story and into the world of the gospel, and is interpreted by it. It is no longer a dream to be dismissed as an illusion or mere fiction. This dream reveals truth, a word from God for Anna. That, at least, is the suggestion of the chaplain in linking Anna's experience with this Bible story. She does not claim that this is indeed the case or that it is the only valid interpretation. That is the topic of the conversation God himself must have with Anna. The chaplain's job is simply to make the suggestion. She does not fill the space between Anna and the Eternal One by forcing her interpretation upon Anna but simply tells the story. It will not immediately be clear whether this interpretation will have a transformative effect. Only at the very end do we feel that something has happened. Anna remains a mother and does not allow this status to be taken away from her. The woman who was raped and abused as a girl, while nobody came to her rescue or even noticed what was happening, discovers in herself the possibility for the kind of unconditional acceptance she never knew as a girl.

A sound doctrine of sin

In her dream Anna found the courage to break through the chain of rejection that marked her life, and in her conversation with the chaplain some of that joy came to surface. From a theological angle this brings us to the concept of sin. Theologians have given much thought to the subject, not from a sense of pessimism but out of the realism of faith. A sound doctrine of sin encourages a kind of realism that looks at the world from the perspective of divine grace. Sin and evil are not ignored, but neither are they regarded as absolutes. The Christian doctrine of sin—however unpopular or hated the concept may be—has provided us with a fine fabric of differentiations that can be used in pastoral and spiritual care to sort out the kind of situation that is at hand. In Anna's case it helps to recognize one characteristic of sin, namely, that a person may use other human beings or even make them into their prey. This has happened in Anna's life. She was prey. Or to use a technical term: she was the object of instrumentalization.

Breaking the chain

In many instances the word "sin" has little meaning. It is too general. We have to conjugate the verb and explore and define the various forms of sin that we find. Often we come upon patterns of evil that will persist across generations, unless the chain is broken at some point. The story of Anna is a link in a tale of many generations of incest, neglect, and rejection. The family-systems theory of the Hungarian-American psychiatrist and psychotherapist Ivan Boszormenyi-Nagy may help us to throw some light on what theology refers to as "original sin."[2]

The concept of original sin concerns an experience that is all too evident in our society, in world history, and in many individual lives. We are parts of constructs and patterns that cause evil and damage. We have a great deal of trouble breaking these bonds, whatever we do and whatever our good intentions may be. The ways we arrange our lives, what we expect

---

2. Boszormenyi-Nagy, *Foundations of Contextual Therapy*. For a fuller discussion of original sin, Van der Kooi and Van den Brink, *Christian Dogmatics*, 318–24.

from relationships, how we take our children's partners into our family; how we carry on secret addictions, our eating habits: these are all, to a greater or lesser degree, parts of patterns and developments that continue to make new victims. Like it or not, we participate in a worldwide web of evil through the choices we make about our food, by involuntarily supporting child labor, or as a result of the pollution that ends up in lakes and oceans courtesy of our washing machines. In cases of incest and neglect, like Anna's, we quite often see how the victims themselves become perpetrators, causing the pattern to continue. Or, as a psychiatrist described the train of woe: it continues unless a child steps up to break it. But this often proves to be impossible, beyond human capabilities.

The psychiatrist who made that statement was not aware of how these words affected the chaplain. It caused an unexpected sense of joy and insight: "I live with the story that there *was* such a Child who stepped forward to break the bonds."

There is a moment in Anna's dream in which she is overcome by another dynamic, one stronger than her initial intentions. In her dream *acceptance* surpassed her sense of *hurt*. Just as in the parable of the welcoming father, there is no reproach when her son stands before her. Something else breaks through: love and grace. It is therefore hardly surprising that "interruption" has become one of the popular ways to describe grace. Grace breaks through, intervenes. Something new appears that is stronger than what came before.[3] That is why grace may be called "new." Something like this happened to Anna. She sees something that she had not known before.

Anna is the opposite of the father in the first story. His scolding of his son-in-law was more or less understandable. The father was furious because his son-in-law had deserted his daughter. Never again will he allow him to enter his house. The father feels his attitude is fully justified. He has given his son-in-law a job, introduced him to a Bible study group, played a role in his conversion—and now, in spite of it all, this happens. Nonetheless the question arises about the core issue here. Is it about his efforts for this son-in-law, or the son-in-law himself? Had the son-in-law become a mere project, a means to order and control the world of his daughter and, thereby, of himself? Perhaps things started as a mixture of these two elements, but the balance had tipped via this one underlying thought: Just leave if you do not want to be what I intended you to become.

---

3. Van der Kooi and Van den Brink, *Christian Dogmatics*, 160–62.

Human experiences, like motherhood and fatherhood, may at their best moments become windows on God: moments of concern, of acceptance, and later also of trustingly letting go. In Anna's dream we notice something that in the history of theology has been labeled as "justification." This concept of the "justification of the sinner" tries to say that God finds reasons within himself not to abandon humans beings but to maintain and restore his connection with them. God does this "apart from the law" (Rom 3:21), that is, without steps or conditions that we would consider reasonable. Justification means that a new start is made, is offered, without any preconditions. This breaks through in Anna's dream.

A new beginning

The church sees this new start, the breaking of the chain of death and evil, in Jesus of Nazareth. In his life, in his interaction with people, and even in his death and resurrection, we see God's fundamental concern for Israel confirmed and made concrete. God wants to live, and to establish his name, among the people. Paul summarizes the significance of Jesus Christ in the long history of the covenant in one word: God says "yes" to humanity, to his entire creation, and not "no" (2 Cor 1:19). In other words: in Jesus Christ God's intention and promise for the world are realized and carry on. When Jesus appears, the satanic spiral of misfortune, tragedy, evil, and fate is broken through. The story of the temptations in the wilderness reveals this in a few short sketches (Matt 4:1–11). Jesus is led by the Holy Spirit (!) to the wilderness where he hears a series of voices that are difficult to identify. All these voices offer appealing solutions: stilling hunger, achieving popularity, and winning power over the world. In three consecutive scenes we see how Jesus is able to discern these voices, maintains his trust in God, perseveres, and thus shows who he is. In this resistance to the great deceiver, we see a prelude to Jesus' breaking of the bonds of evil throughout his life, culminating with the apotheosis of the cross and the resurrection.

Easter confirms the breaking of these chains and spreads its glory any time someone steps up to do the same. The light of Easter penetrates very far. J. R. R. Tolkien argues that this is the reason why fairy tales and myths, in which evil does not win but life and hope are on offer, sound a distant echo of the good news of the Bible.

God makes new beginnings: we see something of this emerging in Anna's dream. Protestant theology refers to the new beginning that God initiates for the benefit of humankind as justification. The vagabond is welcomed as a son or daughter. Not that this is all there is to say about the interaction between God and us. We might hope that those who have experienced such a welcome and are allowed to join the party will themselves take steps to respond to this generosity in kind. In theological language we call such steps sanctification, or (if that word seems too smug) transformation, deep and full change. Besides, this homecoming with God, this reinstatement as a son or daughter, will require some real effort. We refer to this as reconciliation. Reconciliation encompasses a broad process of restoration. It demands certain steps; it takes time and effort. And even then, it may be beyond one's reach.

Big words: forgiveness and reconciliation

What is the meaning of words like "forgiveness" and "reconciliation" in light of the later e-mails of Anna, in which she declares her inability to forgive the men who hurt her so deeply? Should Anna forgive them? Is that the measure and the purpose of the gospel and of various therapies? For Anna, and many others, this is asking too much. She cannot do it. None of the perpetrators ever acknowledged what they did, and in all probability they never will. In such situations it is crucial to have a clear idea of what the concepts of forgiveness and reconciliation might mean. Within the limits of this book we cannot provide full detail, only give a few suggestions that may help us to think this through.

First, given the long, intense reflection theologians have devoted to these concepts, it is far from easy to bring all the strands of reconciliation and forgiveness under one umbrella. If we have to do so, we would choose the umbrella of salvation, of restoration, of reaching a point where broken relationships have been healed because evil has been acknowledged and removed. Second, by speaking in such broad terms and taking restoration as the umbrella, we have already indicated that there are no easy solutions. In our terminology we must carefully distinguish between forgiveness and reconciliation. Forgiveness represents the first step, in which the other is freed from his guilt. However, this is just a first step and in many cases must be followed by something else. We might refer to that next step as reconciliation. Again, reconciliation is a process, a way of beginning a phase in our lives in which trust and mutual bonding may grow. The perpetrator or the person who was guilty of something evil has the chance to show that he is prepared to once again resume his due place in life. This is very much like Anselm's theory of atonement, that is, atonement through satisfaction.[4]

None of this is at hand in Anna's story. There is no acknowledgment of responsibility on the part of the perpetrators—not even one of them— and for her it is beyond her power, many bridges too far, to take a step of forgiveness without first hearing this acknowledgment. A well-known example on the other side is that of Corrie ten Boom, who forgave the camp commander who was one of those responsible for the death of her sister Betsie. Corrie ten Boom was able to forgive because for her the forgiveness she had received from God in Jesus Christ was all-decisive. We might call this a form of Sermon-on-the Mount Christianity: since you have received pardon for your guilt, you can forgive the other who asks for the same pardon. Karl Barth's doctrine of atonement is a variant on this pattern. In Christ God reconciled the world to himself and as a result we can now see earthly situations of injustice and guilt in that light, and act accordingly. Does this mean that the *possibility* to forgive carries the *obligation* to forgive? Corrie ten Boom was able to do so, but should this really be required of everyone?

Theology must not too easily use such big words as "reconciliation" and "forgiveness." As soon as they are abstracted from concrete situations, there is a good chance of not doing justice to concrete inter-human relationships but of using the gospel in a cheap manner. It is not only important that the victim take a step but, even more, that the perpetrator(s) change their ways and acknowledge what they did. That will open a road towards restoration. And this requires time. To put it in pneumatological terms: the work of the Spirit takes time.

Hand it over to God

Often this will not happen, either in personal relationships or in a collective perspective. Or it may come about but only very slowly.[5] How much effort and how many years has it taken for Americans to begin to acknowledge the injustices and devastation wrought upon native peoples and African Americans in their history? Most of us can tell of our own experiences of broken relationships among family or friends that apparently cannot be

---

4. Van der Kooi and Van den Brink, *Christian Dogmatics*, 461–67.

5. See the examples given by Kellenbach in her impressive book, *The Mark of Cain*.

restored. In real life stubbornness, blindness, powerlessness, or just plain laziness often prevails.

Because of all this the chaplain points to another perspective. It is the perspective of eschatology and divine judgment. She encourages Anna to hand matters, including her own powerlessness, over to God. She connects her abusers' lack of acknowledgment of their evil deeds with God's wrath. In other words: God has not finished with this business. The word "wrath" may not be a popular term, but it has solid theological credentials. It is often needed in the work of the pastor. It does justice to people and their experiences.

The most profound word and the biggest turn-around, however, comes from the other side. The medieval painter Matthias Grünewald pictured this in an impressive way on the Isenheim altarpiece, which is now in the Unterlinden Museum in Colmar, France. The central panel of this triptych portrays John the Baptist, who points his finger to the crucified Christ. It is accompanied by the words of John 1:29: "Behold, the Lamb of God who takes away the sin of the world." One small detail provides a fitting end to our reflections here. Back in the Middle Ages this triptych was found in a hospital, and the smallpox that covered the crucified Christ were the same as those of the patients in this hospital who were dying from it.

Chapter 4

We Are Yours, Evil as We Are
On Sin and Covenant

O MAN, THY GRIEVOUS SIN BEWAIL

ON MY WAY TO the hospital I listen to the car radio. Today there's an interview with a victimologist, someone who studies the experiences of crime victims. The discussion centers on a question one of her students had posed: Are women capable of the same cruelties as men? The expert says that, after many years of study, she must admit that under extreme circumstances, and in specific contexts, all people are capable of terrible things.

It makes me sigh. It is an awful conclusion, but to be honest, it is nothing new. We are "inclined" toward all kinds of evil—I did not learn this at home but heard it from a childhood girlfriend who belonged to a rather conservative branch of the Reformed faith. It's right there in the Heidelberg Catechism. Now the authors of that doctrinal manual observed the criterion that everything in the Catechism had to provide comfort. They said so already in their first lines: "What is your only comfort in life and in death?"[1] It might be hard to imagine, or easy to forget, a catechism as a book of comfort! It's especially hard at this point.

"Inclined towards all evil." Not having been raised in a church environment, I'd like to correct the men who wrote that and change the wording

---

1. *The Heidelberg Catechism*, Lord's Day 1, Q/A 1, 69.

to "capable of." That would give a little more space for all the good things in our lives as well as the bad things that happen.

This was very aptly expressed in the sermon the pastor of the Thomaskirche in Leipzig gave to an overflow audience on the Saturday afternoon after the crash of the German airplane on March 24, 2015. The pilot had intentionally flown the plane into a mountain. We had gone to hear a Bach cantata, but the event unexpectedly assumed the character of a memorial service. "O Mensch, bewein dein Sünde groß"[2] (O man, thy grievous sin bewail)—so the choir sang in the church where Bach worked as cantor for twenty-seven years. The pastor then read the text, Luke 11, which tells the story of Jesus exorcising demons. "This is a brave man," we whispered to each other.

Each sentence hit home. Every seat in the church was taken, but there was total silence. "Widerstehe doch der Sünde," the choir sang, and this summarized the content of the sermon. Resist sin, resist the possibility of sin, be trustworthy for those entrusted to you, accept your responsibility, confront the voice of the Deceiver, do not give him any foothold.

I could not help but think of President George W. Bush who, after the attacks of 9/11, had pointed away from himself to others, fulminating against "the axis of evil" and then piously reading Psalm 23. It is a beautiful psalm, but Bush missed the point. He chose a path that was too easy and so self-satisfying: it is the others, and not we ourselves, who are dangerous and represent evil.

This puts us at ease: evil is outside of ourselves, with others. But the Heidelberg Catechism and Pastor Amberg of the Thomaskirche make it something much more frightening. Evil, the possibility of committing evil acts, is nearby. We, you and I, should not lend our ears to promptings to do evil. Just recognize its nearness and do not be surprised—this is not something foreign to you.

The possibility of doing evil things lies within all of us, and we can only resist it if we dare to look it in the face. The church has known this for a long time and does not need to undertake any new, significant studies on the matter. Rather, the church has a sound piece of advice: resist evil and manifest love.

2. J. S. Bach, *Matthäus Passion,* BWV 244.

THE GRIEVING OLD WOMAN

I had to think of all these things as I sat at the bedside of an old woman. I visited her in the hospital shortly after our experience at the Thomaskirche. Her hospitalization had opened up a lot of grief—a grief so overwhelming that she had put it on hold for some time. This is what we sometimes do: when faced with great sadness, we may not have any tears because we know that once this grief has erupted, we will not have tears enough. "My heart felt like a stone," the old woman said. "How was it possible that I did not cry for such a long time? I am not an uncaring person." Her eyes were as blue as the skies. "But now that I am here, in this building where my husband died, now that I meet the same nurses who cared for him, and now that I see you again, it seems that everything is released. It is difficult but it also gives relief."

"Just tell me," I said.

And so she did. Her son had been imprisoned for incest. "This is so terrible, and it will never go away. Our family has been scathed forever; it is unbearable. But I love my son, I can't help it. People tell me: naturally, you will never want to see him again. But he is and remains my child, and I will always love him. Some people refuse to have any further contact with me because I don't tell my son not to come by anymore. But I know there is good and evil in him, just as in myself. Just as in all of us. Should I reject him? What he did should never have happened; I am not defending it. But is he more evil than I? You understand what I am saying?"

"If I hear you correctly, you are saying two things. That you, despite everything, will always be his mother. And, more specifically, you touch upon a profound Christian awareness that none of us is without sin and that, therefore, you must not judge him. You condemn what he did, not who he is. You are in the good company of Jesus when the people wanted to stone the adulterous woman. 'Anyone who is without sin may throw the first stone,' he said. One after another the crowd bows before that word. This truly gives relief: we do not have to sit in judgment on people. That is God's job. Love is fulfilling the law. That gives us plenty to do."

She looked me straight in the face. There was nothing more to be said.
Reflection

Sin and unease

"Sin" is not a popular word. It is mainly used in church, and even there it is avoided as much as possible. Sin evokes weight and responsibility, an unacceptable burden, something smelling of the past. And, therefore, we dodge around this theme a lot. This is understandable from a psychological as well as from a theological point of view. We prefer to keep guilt and responsibility at a distance. But the story at the start of this chapter refers to an episode in which concepts like sin and guilt become unavoidable—and helpful. There was no way of denying that the crash of Germanwings Flight 9525 on March 24, 2015, was no accident, but a conscious and probably desperate act of a copilot who presumably wanted to ensure that his name would live forever in the annals of history. He locked the other pilot out of the cockpit and flew the plane with all its passengers and crew into a mountainside. The service in the Thomaskirche in Leipzig was an example of how, from both a religious and therapeutic point of view, the liturgy ought to function in a sound church service. In this case, not just the ambiance of this monumental church or the magnificent music but every sentence in the sermon hit home. At the basis of it all was a theology attentive to the reality of evil committed intentionally and after careful consideration. The sermon stood out by not pinning the reality of guilt and evil only on the pilot. Rather, it involved the entire church community. Not that the audience was declared guilty but that we were reminded of how frightfully close doing evil may be. We live in a world in which doing evil as well as good is just around the corner. This may sound rather pessimistic, but that is not the case. To accept that the possibility of evil is deeply entrenched in our world and that we cannot distance ourselves from it is to gain breathing space. It is to recognize that demons and evil spirits are not only figures in an ancient worldview but may suddenly be detected right around us, in our own present moment.

One implication is that we will sometimes be collectively blind to this fact and come to recognize it only later. An individual, but more often a group of people, an entire social class or nation, may be bewitched by something big that we recognize only in retrospect as an idol or demon. In such a case we do not use the word "demon" to locate evil outside of ourselves but to affirm that we are more frequently blinded or possessed than we care to admit. This happened in Germany in the 1930s, when an entire nation followed a democratically elected leader in search of a toxic ideal compounded of racism, economic hunger, and extreme nationalism.

We can find more than enough evidence of embodiments of evil in our own time. Just think of the practices of ISIS, when children were used to kill, prisoners of war slaughtered, and everything justified by an appeal to Islam. Or closer to home: think of how bankers' greed and social irresponsibility fed the financial meltdown of 2008 and all the losses that ensued. And how will we, or our children, look back on the toxic nationalism now being proclaimed in the name of "the people"?

Limited self-knowledge

One characteristic of a world that "lies in sin" is that our self-knowledge is limited. We cannot step outside ourselves and arrive at perfect judgments and opinions. This was the ideal of the long-cherished Enlightenment, an ideal that continues to live on among many people. *We* are reasonable, *we* know ourselves, *we* have found (at least the blueprint for) the best kind of society, the best culture, and are thus beyond any justified accusation.[3]

For this reason, a healthy doctrine of sin is so important and liberating. It enables us to detect our own role in this world and to sharpen our eye for the moments that really count without being overcome by them. We do not need to give further examples of the opportunities of doing evil that may come our way. We feel ashamed just mentioning them. At times they become reality, as in the case of Germanwings. In such a situation the text and the music of the Bach chorale is extremely relevant: "Widerstehe doch der Sünde" ("Ne'er Let Sin O'er Power Thee"). This does not surrender us to defeatism but reminds us of our situation and keeps our feet planted firmly on the ground. In this world evil must be resisted, and people must learn how. In the case of the old woman and her son, the patient has become aware of this challenge and this gives direction and ground to her love.

"Capable of all evil"

The chaplain in this story suggests an interesting correction in the text of the Heidelberg Catechism. She proposes that it should read "*capable* of all evil" instead of "*inclined* towards all evil." This makes sense for the term

3 The syndrome is clear Left, Right, and Center in American discourse—from woke self-righteousness to Lloyd C. Blankfein, CEO of Goldman Sachs, saying that bankers under neoliberalism are doing "the work of God," to Donald Trump's endless exaltations of White nationalism.

"inclined to" quickly leads us to think of a constant predisposition toward or a constant trait of evil in our psyche. This is implausible in that we find so many moments in ourselves and in people around us of genuine goodness and of the joy that results from this goodness. Here perhaps is a difference with the time of the framers of the Catechism. It was not their intention to describe a spiritual state of affairs that infects human life in its entirety. Rather, we live in an environment in which evil may suddenly throw itself upon us. Still, a one-sided psychological application of the Catechism may lead to morose and insoluble feelings of guilt.

Blood is thicker than water: on God and the covenant

The third scene of the mother in hospital is very enlightening from a theological perspective. The son has committed incest. He has caused a lot of misery, much of it irreparable. Incest, sexual abuse, is theft. It causes an alienation of one's person, of wholeness, of integrity. Some things may be pushed away by the spirit but are not forgotten by the body, as many victims of abuse know. The mother fully accepts this. Nonetheless, her son remains her child. She does not want to, and cannot, reject him. She thereby reflects characteristics that the Old Testament attributes to God. Jeremiah 31 describes God as a woman who sees how her children are taken from her and who is overcome with grief: "How could I forget you?" Such images and words remind us of the covenant, or, more precisely, the covenant with Abraham that is mentioned several times in Genesis. The covenant at Sinai, in which the law of Moses is given to Israel as a norm to adhere to, elaborates this covenant but is not identical with it. When in moments of crisis the Sinaitic covenant is broken, God falls back on the covenant with Abraham. For God cannot abandon this people, his son. This does not mean that the evil committed is ignored. On the contrary, its reality is recognized. This brings us to the doctrine of God. Christian theology does not define God as a neutral supreme power. God is a passionate God. The mother does not give up on her child, in spite of her grief. Love finds back-channels in which to flow. This is portrayed in the story of the Good Shepherd who goes in search of the one sheep that has become separated from the fold and is lost.[4] Blood is thicker than water.

The mother has an additional reason for not turning her son away, a reason that goes even deeper: Am I a better person than he is, she asks? This

4. Matthew 18:12–14; Luke 15:3–5.

awareness should always be present in a pastoral encounter, and the model of the Good Shepherd should provide the guiding principle. Pastoral care is a form of spiritual care, but the two concepts are not identical. A spiritual caregiver who knows about the Good Shepherd, a *pastor bonus*, casts the situation in the light of this Shepherd. It guides us in the way we take sin and guilt seriously while not allowing it to assume total control. The mother in the story not only stands with her son because of her love for him but also because she knows who she is herself. The title of a book by the Roman Catholic priest Kristiaan Depoortere puts it perfectly: *We Belong to You, With All The Evil That We Bring Along.*

Chapter 5

Ibrahim

On the Strangeness of God

A NEW NURSE HAS come to work in our psychiatric ward. Dark eyes, calm expression. He introduces himself to me. Firm handshake, pleasant voice.

"Ibrahim, I am a temporary worker," he says.

"I am one of the two pastoral workers here," I reply. "The chaplain," I add, noticing that he did not quite understand what I said.

Now he does: "Ah, the pastor! Coffee? We have a quiet evening. Please, tell me what you do . . ."

A nurse who is curious about my work! This happens rather often on the outside. Somehow I seem to carry the romantic aura of the hospital. People say: "It must be difficult work!" Or: "What a unique opportunity to tell people in their last moments about the gospel!" I find it difficult to find right words in such situations. I know my words often disappoint people and I prefer them to be fond of me.

Inside the hospital, however, our job seems much less romantic, and it's quite rare to be asked so cordially to tell something about my work.

The worst thing is when people base their ideas of our work on things they heard or experienced in the past, and that does not always make me happy. But I am glad for Ibrahim's sincere and unexpected interest. I sit down and accept the coffee. Sometime ago I read a statement by C. S. Lewis which I have seen ever since as an invitation and commission: "A Christian is freer to appreciate the good things in other religions than an atheist is."

Thus I enter into a conversation with a young, attentive nurse, whose faith is based on another Book.

"We have much in common," he explains. "Take my name, for example. It stems from an old person in your Bible, whom we also have in our Qur'an."

"You seem to know a lot about these things," I say. "Did you learn that at home? Are you a practicing Muslim?"

"No," he replies, "that will have to wait. The moment I decide to be a Muslim, I must live like a Muslim, and I am not ready for that. You see, that is something I find rather odd with you Christians: you say that you are a Christian, but you live like anyone else. Drinking, smoking, sex, dishonoring your parents—I cannot understand this. I have friends who tell me they are Christians, but they do everything their faith tells them not to do. I also do these things, but that is why I'm waiting awhile before I convert. You Christians say that God will forgive you, and therefore you feel free to do what you want. You say one thing and do something else. I hope I do not offend you, but for me Christianity seems very illogical. With us you know what is expected of you, what you are supposed to do, and what you will receive as a reward. But you have a gentle God who never gets angry and is willing to ignore everything. I don't get that. We take our religion much more seriously. I will wait until I am thirty and then I will become a real Muslim." And, with a cheerful wink: "I will first have some fun."

"It is good to see that you are serious about the faith of your parents," I say. "That is the right thing to do. Important things are at stake. *No words, but action*, as the fans of [Rotterdam soccer club] Feyenoord sing. You would be able to join them in their songs."

He grins. "I don't like soccer. But the song is okay."

DEBRIEFING IBRAHIM

What a pleasant, intelligent person! I must admit that the Christian faith is strange and illogical. The God I believe in does not ignore anything. Yet there is a "wonderful exchange" from which we benefit. Whether or not I am a beloved child of God does not depend on my good deeds. He simply gives, *pro Deo*. I am at a loss to explain this. He is a God who goes out of his way to search me out, a God who "cloth'd himselfe in vile mans flesh, that so / Hee might be weake enough to suffer woe," as John Donne put it.[1]

1. Donne, "Divine Poems XI," in Donne, *Complete English Poems*, 441.

He is a God who, being crucified, holds this whole terrible and delightful world in his grip.

You cannot invent such a God. If I were to invent a God, it would be a God like Ibrahim's: a tit-for-tat kind of God. I will do what he demands from me, and he will reward me by giving me the status of his child who is entitled to a place in heaven. A kind of green-grocer's God. That is a God I can understand. Logical. Totally just and reasonable.

Ibrahim is right when he says that saying one thing and doing something else produces friction. He seems a decent person, is consistent, and he perceives that Christianity opts for another route than Islam, even though he finds that difficult to accept.

A little later I heard a joke that fits well with this conversation.

A person has died and knocks at the gate of heaven. Peter answers.

"What do you want?" Peter asks.

"I want to come in."

"That will cost you one hundred points," Peter calculates for him.

"Yes, but I always attended church."

"Okay. Two points."

"And, eh, I made regular donations to different charities."

"Excellent. Two more points."

"And . . . I was always faithful to my wife, even in my thoughts."

"Another two points," Peter responds generously.

"But, this way, I will never have enough points!" the dead man exclaims in fear.

"Come in." Peter says.[2]

An intense conversation developed during this quiet evening between Ibrahim and the chaplain. Unfortunately, Ibrahim did not become a permanent employee. I would have loved to work with him and one day to have shared this joke with him.

---

2. I told his joke once from the pulpit in my hospital. One of the female members of the choir commented very audibly: "That must be worth at least one hundred points." For a few moments this remark created a hilarious atmosphere.

REFLECTION

New segregation and compartmentalization

We live in pluralistic societies. This is a nice term for a situation we have not yet become fully accustomed to. Our societies do not consist of one big circle with one center, but of a multitude of circles that partly overlap. Many of these circles do not even touch each other and know nothing of each other. This is also true with respect to faith and religion. Knowledge of other religions that have some presence in our countries (Christianity, Islam, Judaism, Hinduism, and Buddhism) is rare, at least knowledge in any depth beyond a few generalities and prejudices. There is a lot of diversity, also within each of these religions. Travel opportunities, long-distance vacations, the internet, Google, Facebook, Twitter, and YouTube help us come into contact with one another, and thus to be part of a big world. But does that mean we really know this world? To some extent, yes: we travel to far-away places, we receive all kinds of information almost instantly, and we seem to face infinite opportunities. However, experiential knowledge, acquired through reading, thinking, and personal encounter, is often sadly lacking. A tourist remains a tourist. He knows that he will go home again in ten days. We live in our own circles, our own neighborhood, with our own colleagues and friends, in our own social layer, with our own particular language and perspective. We might refer to this as segregation and compartmentalization. Not just along the lines of religious connection, but even more in the matrices that play a more prominent role in society: the workplace, our neighborhood, our recreation, the music of our band or choir that demands so much time. All these domains determine to some extent the way in which we look at, and think about, our world.

The conversation with Ibrahim confronts us with this social complexity. This has become daily routine for chaplains and spiritual coaches but, compared to just a few decades ago, it is a totally new experience. Often, standard theology and theological students are hardly, if at all, prepared for this. Their kit is often dated and needs some new tools.

It helps to recognize that the opportunity of meeting someone like Ibrahim is relatively recent. He belongs to the band of well-educated citizens, the second generation of an immigrant group. So he grew up in a pluriform culture even if he has no idea of what a chaplain is or does. Yet, at the same time, the very name "Ibrahim" rings a religious bell. In the past this name was rare in our society even if one of the most famous American presidents bore its cognate, Abraham. We may have sat next to James at school without realizing that the name was derived from the ancient biblical story of Jacob, the son of Isaac. We are nowadays much more aware that we have other living religions around us besides Christianity. The first step to take in our theology, therefore, is a change in our self-perception.

The dominant theology in the post-World War II era operated in a situation in which our countries were still defined by their Christian heritage. With a few exceptions the theologians and pastors of the nineteenth and twentieth century lived with the sense of being in a majority position—culturally, politically, and with regard to worldview. This is no longer the case. In the Netherlands, for instance, the report "God in Nederland," published in 2016, shows an enormous decline in religious involvement.[3] In the US, self-identified Christians dropped from 77 to 65 percent of the population between 2008 and 2018, while the religiously unaffiliated share rose from 17 to 26 percent.[4] Many no longer have any, or only a minimal, knowledge of the Christian faith. Large groups of people are growing up without any familiarity with Bible stories and know nothing about the Good Samaritan or the Good Shepherd. For many, Christmas and Easter are only about lights or the Easter bunny, let alone Pentecost or Ascension Day. This is not to say that religion has completely disappeared from our societies. In some neighborhoods religion has in fact become more visible, even in a physical sense. The inhabitants of certain sections of major North American cities will most likely be able to point to a number of mosques where men assemble on Friday for evening prayer. But these are not to be found in more expensive (note: not "better") neighborhoods.

The moral perspective

Our chaplain meets Ibrahim. As already mentioned, Ibrahim fits with most of his contemporaries in knowing very little about the Christian faith. His understanding of the faith in which he grew up is also rather limited. He sees faith as a system of obligations and as a particular lifestyle. No casual sex, no alcohol, no smoking. He does not have a high regard for the Christians around him. They are not very meticulous in how they live. Their behavior is totally at odds with what they claim to believe. Christians are quite similar to those who say they do not believe in God or in whatever. In

3. Bernts and Berghujs, "God in Nederland."
4. Pew Forum, "Decline of Christianity."

other words: Ibrahim looks at faith and religion from a moral perspective. Faith has to do with conduct, with morals.

How are we to react when the norm for our assessment of faith is mostly one of morality and conduct? The chaplain does not address this issue. Why not? Implicitly she agrees with Ibrahim, probably because he has a point. Most Christians hardly differ in their way of life from the people around them. The American theologian Stanley Hauerwas has been very influential in stimulating a discussion about the church as a counterculture, in pointed contrast to the dominant modern culture. Is this demand or expectation realistic? The average Christian has to a great extent assimilated to the way of life of his neighborhood. There may perhaps come a time when large groups of Christians will follow a route different from that of their neighbors, but that moment has yet to come. This may be why the German theologian Dietrich Bonhoeffer is so unbelievably popular among Christians of every persuasion. In his life Christian discipleship became visible and concrete.

Once upon a time the situation was different. The first generations of Jesus' followers were so different that they drew the attention of society. They refused to join in the worship of the numerous idols that dotted daily life around them. They did not want to honor the emperor as a son of the gods, which made them a potential threat to the unity and cohesion of the state. They cared for the sick and the weak and had a different attitude towards the handicapped. They did not kill baby girls, which was considered strange and caused irritation. Boys were desirable, but a surplus of girls was not, so they were often abandoned or even drowned. Infanticide was part and parcel of the society in which the early Christians lived. They attracted attention because of their different conduct.[5] Perhaps there is something to be learned here. A Christian ethos is not achieved by simply implementing a set of rules. As Allan Verhey put it: the early Christians lived out of a memory of Jesus.[6] It will have an effect when people are willing to be inspired by a story, the story of Jesus Christ. Of this Bonhoeffer is a powerful example.

5. Hurtado, *Destroyer of the Gods*, 143–89.

6. Verhey, *Remembering Jesus*.

Our view of God

The chaplain does not deal with various issues such as the question of which religion is right, of whether the Bible is true or the Qur'an. She picks up the thread elsewhere and goes right to the heart of the matter. She focuses on her conversation partner's view of God, which turns out to be very moralistic, and she then compares this to the God of the Bible. The guiding principle used by chaplain falls under the doctrine of God. She does not address the question of whether God exists (*an Deus sit*), or what God is (*quid Deus sit*), but starts with *how* God is (*qualis Deus sit*). Can we separate the *that*-question (whether God exists) from the *what*- and *how*-questions (what do you imagine "god" is like)? Classic theology thought it could; Thomas Aquinas treated it as a separate and introductory issue. Most contemporary theology is critical of this approach and maintains that it, at most, leads to a very abstract concept of God as supreme being—a concept far, too far, removed from the way God is portrayed in the Bible. The chaplain may not have considered all these elements when she opted for a focus on who God is. Often we are led—and rightly so—by our intuition, or more precisely, by the experiences we have gained over the years.

According to Ibrahim, the Christian God is prepared to overlook everything, in contrast with Allah, who rewards good deeds and punishes evil. The chaplain comments that this makes God into a green-grocer who weighs everything by the ounce. We will not argue whether or not Ibrahim's view is correct. Islam has many streams and variations, and the Qur'an uses ninety-nine names for Allah that all point to his grace, goodness, and mercy. It is too easy to simply define Islam as a legalistic religion that is only concerned with external rituals. The respect for the Almighty that Muslims manifest in their faith has much in common with Reformed spirituality that stresses God's holiness and wants us to live in the "fear of the Lord." (In this context "fear" does not refer to anxiety or trepidation but to profound respect and awe before God's holiness.)

God has not remained silent

The second aspect in this conversation that is of theological interest and sets the tone is the chaplain's insistence on commonality. This may be due to the fact that traditional Protestant theology was firmly convinced that God has not remained silent toward humanity. This brings up the theme of general revelation, or, rather, God's universality, as already discussed in chapter 2. The word "general" in the composite term "general revelation" can too readily be taken to mean "colorless" or "vague." But traditional theology tried to point in another direction by emphasizing the sense of the majesty and nearness of God to be found in almost all religions. That people can somehow distinguish between good and evil they took as evidence for the constant and irrepressible activity of God in the human spirit. Theologian and missiologist Johan Herman Bavinck discussed this awareness in an impressive way.[7] The universal revelation of God has a relational color, he said. God wants to have a relationship with us, and we sense this even if we often repress it.

When we start in our theology from the idea that God relates to the people around us before we have exchanged a single word with them, it perhaps opens the possibility of initiating a conversation with someone freely and with positive expectations. We are, after all, not the first to enter into a conversation with this human being.

God steps down

In her next step the chaplain introduces the uniqueness and the strangeness of the "Christian" God. It is a God who makes a "wonderful exchange." These words refer to a hymn of Nikolaus Herman and evoke a whole world of faith, spirituality, and theological reflection: "A wonderful exchange he makes, he puts on flesh and blood. Then gives us back in what he takes, his Godhead as our good."[8] These words remind us of the well-known *dictum* of Irenaeus: God became human so that we might become divine. This exchange—Luther called it "joyful"—is expressed in forceful and beautiful words in the traditional Reformed form for the Lord's Supper:

> In the garden, where he was bound that we might be freed from our sins; that he afterwards suffered innumerable reproaches, that we might never be confounded; that he was innocently condemned to death, that we might be acquitted at the judgment-seat of God; yea, that he suffered his blessed body to be nailed on the cross, that he might fix thereon the handwriting of our sins; and hath also taken upon himself the curse due to us, that he might fill us with his blessings: and hath humbled himself unto the deepest

7. Bavinck, *Church between Temple and Mosque.*
8. Nikolaus Herman, "Praise ye the Lord, ye Christians" (1560), stanza 6.

reproach and pains of hell, both in body and soul, on the tree of the cross, when he cried out with a loud voice, "My God, my God! why hast thou forsaken me?" that we might be accepted of God and never be forsaken of him.[9]

Liturgical practices such as baptism and the Lord's Supper are inseparably connected with theology and the daily life of faith. In dogmatics baptism and Eucharist are often discussed in a separate section, for the sake of clarity, but we must always remember that everything belongs together, and that in dealing with one doctrine we must not forget the other. In the sacraments the believers enter a movement, a drama: the story of Jesus Christ, his commitment, death, and dying. Christian theology discerns in this history *who* God is: a God who commits himself, who gives himself in his son Jesus Christ and thereby shows his love, unto the end.

This concept radically differs from many current ideas about God and the gods. Most people, in the past and even in the present, accept that God is high and dwells in heaven. This is common thinking. However, it makes it utterly strange that God would pursue us and share in the *condition humaine*. So also grace remains something strange. That is the point of the joke about collecting points at the heavenly gate. Many begin their journey unconcerned, believing they will get there as long as they do their best. Not until we realize that we are falling short, that we do not give God and others what we owe them, is there an openness for that other element: unexpected and amazing grace.

9. See, for example, PRCA, "Form for the Administration of the Lord's Supper."

Chapter 6

It Was Never Enough
On Religion and Gender

THE WOMAN IN THE bed near the window was almost invisible under the blankets. I decided to say hello. I had recognized her name on the list of patients in our ward. She was the only person with a private room. She welcomed me in. She told me she had been seriously ill and had thought she would not make it, and that this may well have been her unspoken wish too. However, she survived the surgery and was slowly regaining her strength.

After her husband died, thirty years ago, she had continued caring for her stepbrother, with whom she shared her house. As a young boy he had become seriously handicapped when in a bizarre accident his tractor turned over and threw him into a ditch. That was forty years ago, and ever since he had lived with his sister and brother-in-law.

"I am totally exhausted," she said. "When I came to the hospital, it felt as if I would never be able to do anything, and it still feels that way. As if only now I feel how tired I am. I know I must again get on with my life. I will not abandon that man; that is my duty as a Christian and who else, except me, is his neighbor? But I have no idea how I can manage it. As a young boy he was not particularly pleasant, and today he is an angry, pitiful old man. But he did not ask for this accident to happen. I do what I can. Ten years ago I thought that things might become easier once our children were out of the house, even though they also gave much help. He is in and out of hospital all the time, but I do what I can . . ." For a moment she remained silent. "But it is never enough." It is never enough.

I was alert. "This is not some stray remark. I'm thinking there is a long story behind this . . ."

Then she told me her life story. She was an unwanted child of a single teenage mother. Her mother had often complained that her existence was the cause of her own misery. She had always tried to please her mother: "That was the most important task of my life." The next hour she talked, in tears, and angry with herself because of her tears. She talked about her mother's cruelty, about the punishments that came when she had not done her work the way her mother wanted, about the threats, the loneliness. During the first happy years of her marriage it was as if she had been freed from prison. Children came in rapid succession. Then they had taken in her younger stepbrother. "This was more or less expected of us, but it was also something I wanted myself. We knew each other inside and out, and he had not had a very pleasant childhood." But more and more his conduct began to resemble that of her mother. When she had finished her story, I said, "It sounds as if you have worked your entire life in order to prove that you had the right to exist, and to earn a place on earth."

Tears.

"I hear you are acquainted with Bible. Let me tell you a short story from the Bible, from Luke 10. Undoubtedly you know it. It is about two sisters: Martha and Mary."[1]

"I am so sick of that story!" she almost shouted. "I have always worked, and then worked more, and when this story was told in church, it always felt as if Jesus also thinks that what I do is just not good enough."

"Give the story a chance," I said. "I found an explanation that may throw some new light on it." She gave a slight nod, hesitantly. "All right then," she said at last.

"What could that word of Jesus mean that Mary has chosen the better part, the only part that was needed? It cannot possibly mean that he looked down upon domestic work, cleaning, cooking. These things are essential in order that people may come home to a clean, warm, well-ordered place, find clean clothes in the closet, with a meal on the table and something to drink. All these things are essential for welcoming each other. It is unthinkable that Jesus thought these were unnecessary; he benefitted from them himself. So there must be some other secret hidden in this story. This is what I have come to think. Perhaps Mary's secret was that she trusted she could sit down for a moment and listen and could interrupt her work

1. Told in Luke 10:38–42.

because she knew that Jesus loved her for who she *was* and not for what she *did*. Was this perhaps the misunderstanding and the burden that was weighing heavily on Martha? Could it be that she thought she first had to earn Jesus' love by working instead of trusting that she did not have to earn his love but should simply accept it?

"Is that too easy? Far from it. If I have discovered one thing in my work, in my own heart, it is that it is *not* easy to receive, to accept. It implies giving up the illusion that we are self-sufficient. It demands courage to depend on someone else and to trust that this is okay."

We sat silently for some time. Then she said, "Well, that is a rather different way of hearing the story. I will have to give it further thought. It seems as if it would give some air."

Two days later I stepped into her room again. She said: "I am still thinking about this story, for I have lived my entire life on the basis of the pattern I was used to. It's kind of exciting that I might be able to choose a different way."

When the conversation ended, she told me the matter had kept her awake during the night. "Here I am, I said during the night in my prayer, I will move a little bit towards Mary. Perhaps I really don't have to justify my existence."

Here I am, she said. I hear the echo from Genesis 2, where God simply asked: "Man, woman, where are you?"

Here I am.

At that point God can speak and begin something new.

REFLECTION

What role is expected?

This encounter has a number of elements to which the chaplain could react. In the foreground is a psychological reality: a woman who is mentally and psychologically exhausted. A family doctor would probably diagnose her situation as burnout. It looks as if this exhaustion has much to do with the role she thinks she must play as a woman. In other words: the gender perspective is very clearly present. Further, we have the biblical-theological element, namely the impact of the story of Martha and Mary on her life. Finally, the exegesis of this story leads us to a theological element that remains dormant until it touches on our own relationship with God and thus becomes part of our attitude towards God.

It is typical that different elements in concrete encounters interact and cannot be looked at in detachment from each other. They occur in a context of historical and cultural facts. To what extent do these facts impact a conversation? Realizing that we are confronted with a complex situation raises the question of where we may find our point of departure. What will guide the chaplain and how can she provide orientation? Usually we make subconscious choices led by experience and intuition. But what is the role of gender and other social factors in the kind of intervention that is chosen?

Empirical disciplines and theology

This encounter offers a challenge to systematic theology because it demands an answer to the question of the extent to which social circumstances and empirical disciplines, such as sociology and anthropology, must enter into theological consideration. It should be noted that the relationship between these disciplines is quite challenging and cannot easily be solved. The modern university exhibits a wide array of disciplines, and most scholars prefer to stay within the parameters of their own specialty. To put it bluntly: we prefer to remain in our own comfort zone.

In addition there is the matter of mutual estrangement. Scholars in the empirical sciences often look at theologians as aliens and thus often with suspicion and condescension. On the other hand, theologians suspect that sociologists and anthropologists want to reduce all faith expressions to social or anthropological processes and to jettison theology as a non-scientific misfit at the university. They refer to theology as fairy tales or some other term of ridicule.

In recent decades we have seen various reactions to this situation. British theologian Sarah Coakley has laid them out helpfully.[2] A first way out, or rather escape route, for systematic theology is to concentrate on a high church tradition, dismissing empirical approaches as not fitting with a long and venerable history. A second escape route is that of radical orthodoxy: it accuses modernity of defining the world as a closed box and returns to patristic and medieval (i.e., Platonic) approaches in which earthly reality is thought to participate in a higher, divine order. A third way out is to embrace the perspective of older gender studies and use concepts like

2. Coakley, *God, Sexuality, and the Self*, 71–92.

liberation and autonomy to free oneself from the "authoritarian" power of the Bible and tradition. This approach does offer positive connections with the empirical disciplines. But all three options have the disadvantage of not entering into any genuine relationship with the things empirical science has to offer.

In the encounter described above we certainly detect a negative and depressing effect of our theological tradition. The woman saw it as her duty to continue caring for her handicapped stepbrother. The role she took on for herself was one of working, caring, and not complaining. She was never finished: "It is never enough!" However hard she worked, however much she tried her best, feeling obliged to care as a Martha, she would never be told that she had chosen the better part. She heard no appreciation for her commitment but only got low marks for being Martha instead of Mary.

Surprisingly, the chaplain does not discuss the unspoken claims that the environment puts on a woman. Not that she is unaware of gender issues, but pastoral work often demands that choices be made. In most cases there is only time and attention for one aspect. The chaplain makes her choice and remains on her own terrain. Her approach is biblical-theological and thereby becomes fully theological. She offers an alternative interpretation to the story of Martha and Mary. Mary is not praised because she sits down and listens, but because she is able to receive. Mary represents openness, the discovery that one of the most difficult aspects of the relationship of a human being with God is to receive appreciation, to be aware of having been found and accepted. This is brought out in a number of places in Christian theology. One well-known site is the doctrine of justification. God accepts us in grace and love, without any prior accomplishments, detached from our works. Grace comes unexpected; it is a gift.

A gift

We find this gift-theme elsewhere in our theology too, namely, in the doctrine of creation. Creation and being a creature have a structural tie with the idea of a gift: life is a gift of God. From the very first, we stand in a relationship with God as those who receive. We do not occupy first place in the order of being but second; compared to God, we are secondary. Our existence has in a radical sense *an eccentric structure*.[3] This means that we

3. The anthropological point of departure is that humans are beings who seek love. Or more profoundly: our deepest being consists of our ability to love. However, we are

as human beings have no bird's eye view of the great questions of our existence. We do not possess divine control. We can easily get anxious when we try to think this through. This is precisely what happens in the story of the snake in paradise. The deceiver sows mistrust and confusion.[4] That is his core business. Is God really good and can he be trusted? Isn't he keeping something hidden from us, something that makes us different from him? When Adam and Eve open themselves to this reasoning, unrest and mistrust in God's goodness enter their hearts. From now on life will be a tangle, a mix of good and evil; innocence, "being unaware of," has disappeared beyond the horizon for good.

In this story we immediately hear words of self-justification, of an unbending attitude. First from Adam, then from Eve. Outside the Garden of Eden we will find it difficult to live from a gift, to be, first of all, a receiver. God is first of all the one who gives, who makes a new beginning.

An unexpected gift also forms the point of several parables, as for instance in the one of the workers who started late in the day and in the one of the Prodigal Son.[5] Such stories and parables emphasize that grace does not come automatically; it comes as a surprise, breaking through established patterns.

What this means—living from God's gift—cannot be summarized in a few lines. It demands a great deal to let it become part and parcel of our own faith experience. In the pastoral encounter in this chapter, we see the struggle to escape from the "never enough" syndrome and to try to be a Mary. It demands time and effort.

---

tempted to think that we can do this easily, yet cannot do so until we have discovered that we are being loved unconditionally. "You did not first love me, but I first loved you" (John 15). If we ignore this and do not get beyond this point, it will be our downfall. Our insatiable need to be loved will get in our way, and we will want to earn everything, very understandably from a psychological perspective but also an impossible challenge. Our whole life becomes a matter of bookkeeping.

There is another way, but it demands submission to the love of the Lord who loves for no reason. We find that difficult to digest. We find it more blessed to give than to receive. That is the characteristic human hubris, which cannot submit and trust that God is the one good God. For a theological anthropology that is completely built around this recognition of eccentricity, see Kelsey, *Eccentric Existence*.

4. For an insightful and hilarious description of how this works, see Lewis, *Screwtape Letters*.

5. It is unfortunate that the parable has become known by that name. With Henri Nouwen and Miroslav Volf, we suggest that it should rather be called the parable of the Welcoming or Merciful Father, for the story is more about the attitude of the father than that of the two sons.

Right here lies the real transformative element in this conversation and its aftermath. The new interpretation of the biblical story of Martha and Mary plays an essential role. It helps the patient reconstruct her own life. In her new constellation she is the one who may live from the kind of life that is given to her, in a space that is allotted to her, in which her existence is grounded in a fundamental *yes* that comes from the other side, from God. She discovers that she no longer needs to justify her existence.

In this new framework the pattern this woman had learned early on unravels. Being an unwanted child, she had been declared guilty by her mother and subconsciously tried to justify her own existence her whole life long. In conversation with the chaplain the voice of the mother, which in fairy tales is often rendered as the figure of a stepmother, is drowned out by another voice: the voice of the Creator, who also is the one who recreates.

Besides the figure of Mary who sits at Jesus' feet we are also reminded of another Mary, the mother of Jesus. She also knew what it meant to receive. At the annunciation of the birth of Jesus she represents the believer. "Here I am," she says. Her statement combines openness and vulnerability. It also implies a readiness to cooperate with grace as God has given it. It is not strange that in contemporary Roman Catholic theology Mary is the symbol of the church. She lives from what she has received.[6]

The unique contribution of theology

The story in this chapter shows how the relationship between theology and practice does not run down a one-way street. Daily life and what the social sciences tell us about it also impact systematic theology. We all live in a particular context, and no theological reflection is possible without taking that into account. The social sciences give us tools to explain what happens between human beings and thus to enlighten us about the complex relationship between structures and mechanisms. With respect to the doctrine of sin, for instance, empirical descriptions prompt us to pay more attention to connections and relationships between generations and to gender-specific role patterns. They push us to include more precise definitions and differentiations in our theology which would not have been possible without their empirical contribution.[7]

6. For closing the gap between Protestant and Roman Catholic doctrine at this point, see Van der Kooi and Van den Brink, *Christian Dogmatics*, 575–76.

7. Van der Kooi and Van den Brink, *Christian Dogmatics*, 322–24.

If the social sciences are of theological interest, we venture to maintain that theology is also of interest for the social sciences. Theology has something to contribute with respect to this woman's experience and what sociology might have to say about it. Theology clarifies and defines realities which are empirically observable from the perspective of God: of salvation, grace, and hope. It adds to what is empirically observable. We might also say: theology sets us and the world in a spotlight that enables us to observe things and people in a different way, namely, as destined for salvation and *shalom*.

Chapter 7

Voices

The Need to Distinguish

NOT A DAY PASSES but I'm reminded for a moment of Lydia. Years ago I visited Philippi in the Greek province of Macedonia. There, near a small river, was the place of prayer where Paul supposedly met Lydia. On a sudden impulse I stooped down and picked up seven small stones from the creek bed. I keep them in a small box with my hairpins. Thus, every morning while I'm fixing my hair I think: Oh, yes, Lydia. "Hi, sister from long ago and far away. You who came before us on this continent in longing and faith. You, who allowed yourself to be beckoned by God."

"Beckoned by God." It is an old-fashioned way of speaking. I used it once as the theme at a hospital church service. I ended my sermon on Lydia by saying that, if we all got together, we would be able to collect many stories about God's "beckonings," traces of where we saw or experienced something of him in our lives. Telling these stories to each another would make for a very special conversation in the hospital restaurant. But even without a story about God's beckoning, everyone would be welcome for coffee after the service.

A hospital is a very special place. I was served at my beck and call.

Lia's voice

Lia had been at that worship service. It meant something very special for her to attend because she liked to see how everyone belonged together. She also loved the singing. She had been treated in our ward for a long time for anxiety disorders and depression, and because she heard voices. One day she had asked me, "Do you have a minute for me?" We looked for a good place to sit in the garden. "I did not grow up as a believer," she began. "I think I was baptized, but then we moved and no longer attended church. My mother was a Catholic, my father does not believe. I am not getting any better, so I'm hoping that faith could perhaps help me."

We look at a bird that is hopping around us. I ask her to tell me something about herself. Eventually she brings it out. "I was fifteen and in high school. I was asked by a teacher to look after his kids. I liked small children and felt honored to be asked. The family had just moved and the garage was still unfinished. He wanted me to see it, and there he grabbed me. I was told to remain silent about this or he would fail me in my exams. I had to keep coming to babysit, and each time the same ritual was repeated. First looking at how far the work on the garage had progressed, and then looking after the children."

"Was there not someone, perhaps your mother," I asked, "who sensed that something was wrong?"

"She was so happy that I had this little job. I did not dare to say anything, as she might think that it was my fault, and I badly wanted to succeed in my exams."

My stomach aches. There was a time when I thought all these stories about abuse were somewhat exaggerated, but after doing this work for thirty-five years, I know better. "Was God also there, when you had to come back time after time to the garage?"

"I called on him, but he was not there."

We agree that she will write a letter to God.

In the following weeks I got to know her as very sweet but poor at establishing boundaries. This job of writing a letter was a good and a bad idea. As she wrote the voices became louder and began to shout. "I must listen to these voices," she says, "because I do not want to miss any of them."

"Whose voice is it," I ask.

"It's my mother's. She died eight years ago. I miss her terribly . . ."

"What does the voice say?"

"That I should walk to the railroad and come to join her."

She pulls at the rubber band around her wrist.

"Would your mother really say that to you? Tell me something about your mother."

"My mother? She was so sweet and so caring. She was always there for me and for my children. I long for her more than I can say."

"Would she really want to take you away from your children? How old are they?"

"Fourteen and sixteen."

"Would she really call you away from your children? Would she want you to be with her rather than have you take care of them? Was that what she was like?"

She hesitates. "No, the children were everything for her. They were more important than anything else."

"In that case," I reply sternly, "you are deceived by that voice. It could never have been the voice of your mother."

She stares at the ground. Then she asks hestatingly, "So, whose voice is it?"

"I would not know. But I do know that you are misled and that you should not listen to that voice. It could be the voice of your own heart because life is so difficult. We must talk about this and you must talk about it with your psychiatrist. But it is not your mother's voice. This means that you should tell the voice, 'Get lost, I want to have nothing to do with you.' And then you may say, 'In the name of Jesus, go away.' This, by the way, is what Jesus did with voices that could not be trusted. They are wolves in sheep's clothing." The way she looks at me shows that she does not understand what I said.

"I am sure you know the fairy tale of the wolf and the seven young goats. The wolf acted as if he was the mother of those goats. He too was a deceiver." I watch the penny drop.

Three days later I see a line in fine handwriting in the book that lies in the meditation room: "Thank you, God, that you have beckoned me. Lia."

REFLECTION

At first sight we may wonder what could be said about this encounter from the perspective of systematic theology. The patient is hospitalized with anxiety disorders. She was abused by a teacher for a long time. Is this not a matter for pastoral psychology? This is certainly true, but several themes that belong to systematic theology play a role in the choice of how to react and intervene. In this case it is the matter of the distinguishing the spirits—in other words, of God's speaking and the guidance of the Holy Spirit.

The unique approach

As always with encounters in such settings, here again it is of the essence to listen carefully to the woman who is telling about her destructive experiences and shares with the chaplain that she hears voices. She identifies one of the voices as her mother's. Reasoning from a psychological angle, we might suggest that she longs for her mother. The mother is in a safe place, and in the midst of the chaos of threatening memories Lia seeks security. Yet it is right and significant that the chaplain does not immediately comment that the voice must be an illusion. That might be the task of the psychiatrist but it is not hers as a chaplain. Of course, it can be expected that a chaplain has some idea as to what the psychiatric diagnosis might be, but she has another role to play. If the chaplain had pronounced a psychological judgment, all communication would have broken down. Lia could have clammed up with the thought: "You see, I am crazy." What the chaplain does is to take the voice seriously from a theological angle. Once again, an approach that takes the language and the (possibly) religious experience with full seriousness and evaluates the matter on that basis without reducing the voices to nothing but a psychological phenomenon. Theology has its own sources and possibilities which have their own value and *may* have a therapeutic or transformative effect. *May*, for this is not self-evident. Experience teaches that many spiritual counselors or chaplains have at times wondered whether it would not have been better to also study psychology. Or perhaps philosophy. Would that not offer more possibilities? Indeed, there is a wide overlap in the knowledge and skills required in these fields. Nonetheless, we would maintain that many questions in life have a religious dimension which demands an approach that is theologically responsible. Philosophy sometimes offers wisdom but quite rarely acceptance of one's fate, and even more seldom comfort. Jewish, Christian, and Islamic theology all point to the idea that we do not find our final fulfillment in ourselves but in surrender to God—that is to say, eccentrically, in God as the gracious Other.

Focus on the content

Together with Lia the chaplain explores what the voice might be. She does not enter into any discussion about whether such a voice is possible but focuses on the *content*, on what the voice says. The voice tells Lia to go to the railroad near the hospital, less than a ten-minute walk away. Obeying the voice would bring rest, a return to the security of the mother. It is of theological interest to note that the conversation does not deal with the possibility of revelations or messages from a deceased person in heaven but that the testing of the sources begins with the content.

Let's discuss a few theological observations regarding this choice. First, the doctrine of revelation, or the matter of theological epistemology, is ignored. "How do you know?" was the question that consumed the energy of an entire generation of theologians from the 1970s to the 1990s. The unspoken assumption was that anyone who spoke about God must first prove that knowledge of God was, in fact, possible. It was an era in which the preliminary questions of theology (the prolegomena) functioned as a black hole into which everything else disappeared.

In her approach the chaplain does not skip these core questions, but by starting with the content she follows a more recent development in theology. That is the second point that we should note. The former approach assumed that it was already clear who or what God is. God was thought to be the highest and most perfect being than whom nothing more perfect was conceivable. That was the basis for the doctrine of God, but this assumption does not take into consideration the God of the Bible, who does not so precisely meet the criteria of perfection. The God of the Bible comes down into this life, turns out to be vulnerable, is in Jesus exposed to death; all this has consequences for how people may think about God. God is the power that combats evil and dares to commit himself to that project. As we wrote earlier, the issues of being and knowing are not to be separated. But in the pastoral encounter it is important to begin with the issue of being: What is our concept of God? What characterizes God?

The intervention invites a third observation. The chaplain seems to accept the possibility of a voice or revelation. We've addressed this matter before but I want to stress it again. In theology in general, and in systematic-theological textbooks in particular, revelation is often further designated as the self-revelation of God—that is, in the singular. The plural *revelations* is avoided. The Bible, however, speaks about various ways in which God has manifested himself and has guided his people: through dreams and visions, through dramatic events, through the Torah, through hymns and intuitions, through a path of sorrow and shame, through people, through Jesus Christ, and through the Holy Spirit. How did this plurality disappear from our view? To put it bluntly: after the Enlightenment, culture and theology no longer dared speak that way. It was too strange to accept that God would speak and make himself known through such unusual means as visions and voices.

But hasn't the appeal to such sources of revelation always been the source of heresies, of fanatics, of so-called prophets and mystics who felt free to claim to be the recipients of heavenly revelations? Take, for instance, the Swedish mystic Emanuel Swedenborg. The manner in which the philosopher Immanuel Kant reacted to him is noteworthy. At first Kant was fascinated by him, but in 1766 he distanced himself from Swedenborg in a critical and scornful essay, "Träume eines Geistessehers" ("Dreams of a Visionary"). This has become typical of the aversion that people in academic circles hold for such unorganized and uncontrollable kinds of religiosity. From the nineteenth century onwards it became customary to speak only of God's *self*-revelation. God did not reveal things about the future; he did not give prophetic assignments or inform us about heavenly situations. No, God reveals only himself, his heart, his love. This view and attitude are still dominant in contemporary theology. We fear burning our fingers by touching the uncontrollable religiosity of so-called fringe groups.

Defining revelation as self-revelation is positive in the sense that it puts the emphasis on the fact that God gives himself. But something is also lost in the process: theology no longer provides us with the tools to recognize the plurality of our experiences of God's acting and speaking. It is no longer possible to note, let alone build on, the fact that God speaks in different ways in the Old and the New Testament. A dream is now only a dream. An intense experience of God's presence is no longer plausible but is easily swept aside with the psychological broom. It is all about God's unique self-revelation in Jesus Christ, which has taken place and is still taking place. Thus, theology—from liberal to conservative—has had difficulty in dealing with voices, with "strange" experiences. It moved around them and away from them. Believers and non-believers alike smell this aversion from afar. They are hesitant about coming forward with strange experiences of God, angels, or demons. People, pastors, doctors, caregivers, the "professionals" won't believe you and will look at you with glazed eyes. They deny the very possibility or put it in the drawer of delusions.

Challenged by real life

At this point we encounter something similar to what we sometimes experience in our garage or at our workbench: we lack certain tools and cannot get our work done. *Revelations* plural form a tool that has lately been in such little use that we gradually lost track of it; it has disappeared. But at this point, and not only here, theology is challenged by real life. It is forced to think through unknown situations and things pushed aside. This involves a complete shift in the frequently assumed relationship between systematic-theological reflection and the practice of faith and daily life. It is usually thought that systematic theology, or dogmatics, describes or even prescribes how daily life must be lived, that there is a one-way street from dogmatics to faith and real life. No wonder that this has made the term "dogmatics" so unpopular, smelling of force and imposed prescriptions. We should leave this approach behind and proceed in the opposite direction. Real life experiences invite us, press us, to think anew.

The appearance of a new subject and the need for renewed thought and study has ample precedent in history. Theological reflection has always occurred in response to questions that come up in the practice of daily life. The debates of the fourth and fifth century about the Trinity and Christology were not about abstract issues but were closely connected with the practices of liturgy and prayer. Ecclesiology, or questions concerning the church, offer a more current example. New technology and social media present a challenge that the church must think through. What do the possibilities of the mobile phone or laptop mean for the phenomenon of church? When people are in contact with each other via Facebook and form a prayer chain, are they "doing church"? The concept of church is theologically much broader than the institution that meets on Sunday as a concrete, visible community. New practices and situations challenge us by providing space to think of "church" as a moving and fluid phenomenon. A large variety of initiatives and events may be recognized as "church" and require theological reconsideration. Again, our natural environment and the challenge of sustainability invite renewed thinking about creation and the role of humans and animals in it, challenging the anthropocentrism of our theology. Should we not think more theocentrically and would that not contribute to a different approach towards creation and our use of natural resources? A third topic that could trigger theological renewal: many people in our society nowadays live to a great age. What do these extra years of life mean? What does theology offer for thinking about this new situation? And is there anything that God is teaching us when we are confronted with so many refugees at our borders? These are not just ethical issues; they confront head-on the task of theological reflection. Theology should be geared to the times, as was the case with Thomas Aquinas, John Calvin, and Jonathan Edwards. They did not just repeat older views.

Back to the story of Lia. We talked about the voice she heard and the question of whether it could indeed have been that of her mother. This led us to the theme of revelation, or God's speaking. Did that happen only in the past? Does God still speak directly, or are preaching and the Bible the only channels? There have always been circles that gave explicit attention to the direct speaking of God, under the guidance of the Holy Spirit; mystics and the practices of the Pentecostal churches certainly knew about this. Yet, the mainstream of the church has kept its distance and has been reluctant to credit this phenomenon, and understandably so in view of the many excesses that have come in its train. It would be all too easy to recite examples.

This reluctance should not be the only response, however. In her approach the chaplain leaves open the possibility that such voices are possible. She focuses on the content. "Would your mother really say something like this?" Then she gives back to Lia what Lia apparently experienced from her mother, namely, an absolute priority on the interests of her child and grandchildren. It is unthinkable that this voice would really come from her mother; it has another, dark origin.

The deceiver

Two things with regard to testing such a voice.

First, in this encounter the chaplain refers to the devil as the deceiver. She uses this image to address a topic that is hardly, if ever, discussed in Western theology, namely, that of the devil or Satan. Is the devil a person, or a negative power that we can only conceive of as a person? The choice we make in pastoral work will in part depend on the context of the person we're ministering to, or, to put it in fancier words, on the symbolic universe of the person we are talking with. People in the Southern hemisphere have no inhibitions about speaking in terms of spirits and demons, while theologians who have studied in the West will be reluctant to do so. The decisive factor is whether the chaplain takes the reality of evil seriously, especially in a theological sense. We may discuss the ontology of evil and the devil, but the decisive theological factor is that God's salvation confronts an opposing power and meets resistance, and that the God of Israel and the Father of Jesus Christ has intervened in that encounter. There is no place here for underestimating, but neither for overestimating, the power of the devil. The chaplain defies the overestimation by calling the devil a deceiver. This labeling maintains the person-like element but also has a relativizing effect. It brings breathing space. The devil is not almighty and is not equal to God in power. His core business is to create confusion. When Jesus enters the picture as the living one, the deceiver will have to yield.

Stories and fairy tales

Secondly, in order to clarify what might be puzzling, the chaplain introduces the fairy tale of the wolf and the seven little goats. Lia knows hardly anything about the Bible. She does not know the gospel stories. So another question emerges from this encounter. What can we fall back upon when people are no longer acquainted with the Bible? In a hospital—as a cross-section of society—one meets more people who know almost nothing about the Bible than people who do know what it is about. Is it legitimate in such circumstances to fall back on fairy tales? This opens the question of the function of stories, fairy tales, mythology, fables, films, and literature in relation to the Bible. J. R. R. Tolkien wrote in a beautiful essay that a good fairy tale is a distant echo of the gospel.

"All great fairy tales," Tolkien says, "contain an element that is also found in the story of Jesus." Tolkien calls that element a "eucatastrophe"—a sudden, unexpected, happy turn of events. The Christian gospel, as well as a good fairy tale, provides us with a glimpse of an underlying truth. The story of Christ determines human history. Never before was a story told that people were so eager to embrace, nor one that so many skeptically inclined people were willing to accept as true because of its persuasiveness. It begins and ends in joy. "All great fairy tales," Tolkien says, "are echoes of a powerful, miraculous story that truly happened: the Christian gospel."[1]

Fairy tales keep alive the hope of a happy ending in the small stories and in the grand story. Those who have read *The Lord of the Rings*, or the stories of C. S. Lewis (*The Chronicles of Narnia* and *The Screwtape Letters*) will recognize this. Movies, good movies, deal with the grand themes of longing and anxiety, of justice, injury, guilt, evil, hope, and despair. That does not make them into gospel stories, but it does make them useful in

1. Tolkien, *Tree and Leaf*, 1.

confronting viewers with questions they face in their own lives. God can meet us through literature, film, and a multitude of modern media.[2] These media themselves do not thereby become a source of the gospel, and certainly no replacement for it. But they may serve as instruments on the path that God journeys with people and may confront them with questions from their own existence that demand attention.

2. Cf. Barsotti and Johnston, *Finding God in the Movies.*

Chapter 8

Is It Never Enough?

Talking with God

I FIRST MET MR. Johnson after he had suffered a cardiac arrest and been admitted to our cardiology ward. A cardiac arrest is always dramatic for the patient and for those around him. And so it was for Mr. Johnson: it happened in the church that he had attended since childhood. Shortly after the service had begun, he felt ill and was revived in time by a nurse who also happened to be in the church. So he was still alive, but he was very confused. His behavior had changed and he cried continuously. The medical team was very concerned about him.

After some weeks he was transferred to a rehabilitation clinic. His situation improved greatly until some new heart problems brought him back to us. The doctor repeatedly told him it was a miracle he had come through this second episode so well. Still, he was facing a serious challenge: heart surgery.

Day after day Mr. Johnson fought with himself and with God. He told us he had gone through some difficult months of rehab, with lots of exercises and much physiotherapy. "But," he said, "I realize it is quite miraculous that I am still alive, can do the things I used to do, and that my brain functions as it should. I am lucky; I could just as well have died."

"A time of grace?" I asked.

"Yes," he replied, "a time of grace! Someone called it 'an injury time-out,' but a time of grace is better."

"Is this time of grace something to be happy about?"

"I don't know," he said. "It may sound ungrateful, but this is what bothers me most: all my life I have done what I could for God and the church. I told my children never to say 'no' when the church needed them. As a church elder I accepted a double assignment. I was working in a construction firm as an accountant. Shortly after my twenty-five-year anniversary in this company I was fired because I refused to get involved in fraudulent activities. This is now twenty-five years ago. It drove me literally crazy that my honesty was rewarded with dismissal. For months I was treated in a psychiatric clinic, unable to control my anger. I was always struggling with God. Now this has happened and I cannot help feeling mistreated by God. As if everything that counted for me in life is of no value. It may sound rather disrespectful, but sometimes I wonder whether I put everything in the wrong basket."

"You had other expectations about things to come," I said.

"Yes, I had very different ideas about my future," he confirmed.

For a while we looked outside. "You are in good company," I said. "This coming Sunday I will preach in the hospital church service. It will be about John the Baptist in prison. If you are there, we might talk about it later. Your wife is also very welcome to come."

He came on Sunday morning, in his bed and with his IV line, along with his wife. We read the story of John the Baptist in prison, the man who was assigned to prepare the way for Jesus.[1] He had prepared for this for years but could actually perform his ministry for only three months. At that point he was imprisoned. He had accused King Herod of sexual misconduct for taking the wife of his brother. While in prison he went through intense struggles: Will I get out of here alive? Did I not put all my eggs in one basket—the wrong basket? Is Jesus really the Messiah or were we expecting someone else? I had anticipated something totally different. John sent his disciples to Jesus to ask these vexing questions. Jesus told them: "Go back and report to John what you hear and see: The lame walk, those who have leprosy are cured, the deaf hear, the dead are raised, and the good news is preached to the poor. Blessed is the man who does not fall away on account of me."

All this sounds very convincing. But these words have a barb. John must have noted it immediately, as he was acquainted with this text—Jesus was quoting from the prophet Isaiah who mentions precisely these

---

1. Matthew 11:2–16.

characteristics of the Messiah.[2] But Jesus leaves out something on Isaiah's list. For Isaiah also said, "This is how you will recognize the Messiah. He will announce release to the prisoners and freedom to those who are in chains." That part must have been ingrained in John's memory and exactly what he hoped for, but Jesus left it out. How awkward and painful! And then those strange words at the end: "Blessed is the man who does not fall away on account of me." We are not told what this message meant for John and whether or not it helped him in his struggles. We are left in uncertainty. What we do know is that he did not leave the prison alive but became a plaything in a monstrous game. This young man must certainly have had another idea of his future.

Dealing with the undeserved

A few days later I visited Mr. Johnson again. He was experiencing complications.

"Why do I have to go through all this? I do not deserve it. It's not fair. What did I do wrong? I did everything, everything for God, always ready to assist in church. Is it never enough?"

This short statement "Is it never enough?" alarmed me. "Explain that to me a bit more," I said. And as sick as he was, he started in on an angry account of his father who had not been happy when he, another son, was born. After three sons he had hoped for a girl, and he had constantly tried to change this little boy into someone else. His father enrolled him in courses he detested, told him he had to get top grades, and intercepted and hid letters from firms that invited him for job interviews.

This little boy was now seventy-four years old, and his father had been dead for fifty years. "Two years ago," he said, "I visited his grave for the first time. My wife suggested it. But I couldn't stay there for even a minute because I was afraid that he would suddenly rise up out of his tomb. I do not understand God at all, and how it all fits together. I do not need to live any longer, whether or not my recovery is a miracle. I am sure you think that is wrong?"

"Let's ask God if you do not understand it," I said. "You want God to tell you how it all fits together, where he is in the whole business. This is about your conversation with God. Your request to God is: 'Take my life, I

2. Isaiah 35:1-10, 61:1-4.

do not want to go on.' Let's close our eyes and listen. Could it be that God will speak?"

He was indeed silent for a few moments. Then he said, "I remember that the doctors said it's a miracle that I am still here. It seems as if God still wants me to be around."

"Oh," I said.

Silence. "Does that mean that you should stay away from this path of 'I give up, please let me go'? That God does not want to have you just yet?"

He hesitated and then nodded.

"You had another question. You talked about injustice and said that you had expected your future to be different. Let's put that question to God." And he prayed, "God, why did this happen? This is not what I deserved, is it?"

Silence again.

I said, "What does God say?"

He replied, "I have to think of John in prison. I see him before my eyes."

I: "You see him sitting there?"

He: "He feels deserted, like someone struggling with God. He had other ideas for his future. Just as I had." And after a pause: "John also failed to understand. What a lonely story. And yet, what a memorable man."

I: "According to Matthew he gets that same recognition from Jesus. He called John 'the greatest of those born of women.' We may not know exactly what is meant by greater or smaller. God turns everything around. But you still had a third question. As to your first question, whether it might be enough now, you were reminded that you have been given a further lease on life. As to your second question, about fairness, you saw John the Baptist. But you had another point: 'God, I do not understand and I cannot go on.'"

We remained silent. For three whole minutes, and that is long. Then he said, "God says: you must have patience."

After a while I said, "Does God tell you to have patience? Are you satisfied with that answer? Is that enough for you?"

"No," he replied, "I already have had so much patience."

"Tell him," I said. "It is not important what I might say; this is about your conversation with God."

And he prayed, "God, this is not enough. Patience! I am exhausted. I am afraid. I am at my wits' end."

Once again there was a moment of silence.

"How does this conversation continue?" I asked. He said, "Do not be afraid. When you fall, I will catch you."

REFLECTION

Three acts

This conversation seems like a play in which the curtains at the back of the stage open up one by one. Act I happens in the hospital as a medical-specialist scene. According to the doctor it is a miracle that the patient is still alive in spite of his advanced age and his serious heart failure. In Act II the first set of curtains parts when the chaplain introduces the term "time of grace," which Mr. Johnson prefers to the label of "injury time-out." Now we discern another scene: a man who for his entire life did his best—at his company, for the church—but who was shown the door when he refused to be involved with questionable things. He wasn't compliant and flexible enough for the bosses, not willing to bend when he was expected to. He feels that he has been unfairly treated by people, but even more so, and much more deeply, by God. Being upright, doing his utmost, without it ever being enough. This last short sentence in the conversation is the door-knob to another room in this conversation: the role of God. The chaplain invites this man, seventy-four years old and physically quite frail, to enter that room. Then the scene changes once again—Act III—and we see a man who has been fighting his father for his whole life. *Has been* fighting? The fight is in fact *still going on*. Unwanted as a boy, he became the project of a father who wanted to change him, to the point that he withheld invitations for job interviews and enrolled him in courses he was not interested in. Mr. Johnson has constantly shown the desired kind of behavior, but now life is taking its revenge on him.

What the chaplain does not do

What does the chaplain do? Not all that much. She does not discuss the role of the father; she does not pity Mr. Johnson for the way he was treated by the construction company; she does not ask questions about psychiatric treatment. She does not analyze the psychological issues between this son and his long-deceased father. Mr. Johnson is a frail man, his time of life may be limited; not all his pain can or should be explored. The chaplain opts for a theological approach by zooming in on his extension of life. She offers the term "time of grace" and invites him to the hospital church service the following Sunday. If he accepts that invitation, the way may be open for a conversation about the questions John the Baptist posed to Jesus. That gives the conversation a spiritual or even pastoral tone which maximizes the ties between Mr. Johnson and the church and also alludes to the mission of the chaplain.

The possibilities of a hospital

Situations differ. In many circumstances the language of faith and God is not a first option, but in this case it is possible. Moreover, this story illustrates the real possibilities of an institution where a worship service is held every Sunday. Its creates added value as the patients or clients, whether physically present or listening to the radio, are involved in a church service: a liturgy, hymns, a sermon, prayer, communion with other patients (and healthy people), possibly a choir, and the benediction. Often family members attend as well. Over the years the service in this hospital has become a place where volunteers and others who live in our town meet. In this situation more value is added when the story of John the Baptist is connected with the life story of Mr. Johnson. He clearly suffers a sense of profound disappointment, of an intense desire to be heard, of deep-seated anger that has taken possession of him through the influence of an authoritarian father.

The conversation

However, the conversation does not become a theological debate. Usually sickness and real life are not the appropriate setting for that. In this situation the theologian in the chaplain is present in the moments of silence, which at certain points suggest ways to move forward. This brings us to the real risk in this process: the chaplain's proposal to enter into conversation with God. The conversation acquires the character of a bibliodrama with psychodramatic elements. Mr. Johnson is the protagonist, the person who initiates the action, the conversation with God. The chaplain is the supervisor, or rather the coach, who gives the opportunity, guides, and listens intently.

So, what happens from a theological perspective? Is this bibliodrama, this psychodrama, a form of guided meditation? Is it a form of "listening prayer," as is practiced in charismatic circles? It is all of this. The determining theological factor is the invitation of the chaplain to enter into conversation with God. That is to say: God as subject. Not God as the projection of our own thoughts, not the struggle with the old father, but with God himself. And this by way of the dramatic story of John the Baptist, who does not hear what he presumably hoped to hear: the promise of delivery from prison. It takes real discernment to know when this path should be tried. It will not work if it is only a trick; if that happens the pastoral contact can easily degenerate into blasphemy. But in a ministerial setting—that is, in a situation when it is clear that the spiritual leader has a mission on behalf of the church—the conversation may take this turn. The chaplain invites her conversation partner to begin talking with the *Pastor Bonus*, the Good Shepherd. It becomes a conversation interspersed with moments of silence, in which objections are allowed. "I have already had so much patience with God." And then the courage to say this to God. "God, this is not enough for me. Patience! I am exhausted, I am afraid, I am at my wits' end." The chaplain proceeds with the confidence that God accepts this. Fortunately, and unexpectedly, this does not coincide with the picture that Mr. Johnson has of his father.

Chapter 9

Secrets

On Sexuality, Desire, and Shame

IT TOOK A LONG time before the man showed up. He had wanted me to visit, and the nurse on the cardiology ward thought that was a good idea. "He is very worried about his surgery," she had said. "He said that he wanted to spend some time at home, but that is too risky. It will be good for him to talk about whatever is going on inside him."

But that was not about the surgery. At least, we did not start our conversation there. He avoided the topic for quite a while. He seemed to go off in all sorts of directions: about his wife, his dog, the church that he no longer attended; the church building where he had been baptized and married and that now was sold because of high maintenance costs. It was about his doctor and hospital food. It seemed as if he was trying me out, and I wondered how I could get our conversation really going, for I sensed there was something important at stake. "Would you prefer that we talk somewhere else?" I asked. If there was indeed something major going on, it could be that he did not want others to hear what he said. As chaplain you do not usually start a conversation with the question of whether another place would be preferable, as if you think that this talk will take up major issues when, in fact, you hardly know each other yet. It takes courage to ask, after the conversation has started: "Would you prefer that we talk somewhere else?"

It was a good thing I asked; he immediately agreed. In the family room, where the walls have no ears, he stated the real reason for asking to have this talk. He was very worried that he would not survive the surgery. "I'm not worried that I might die, but what would they do with my computer."

"You are worried about what is on it?" I guessed. He nodded solemnly. "I recently heard that they can trace any site you have ever visited. And I would not want that to happen."

"Tell me more," I said.

"I want to go home before the operation so that I can get rid of the computer. I do not want my wife and my son to explore my life. I have visited sites . . . well, you will probably find this wrong, and maybe God too, but that is not my concern at this moment. I think I may be able to explain it to God. He has created so much beauty. He must have enjoyed himself when he made beautiful people. But my wife will not even want to have my photo on the mantelpiece if she finds out, and my son is such a fussy man, so full of principles. He has no eye for women. What is this in our family? I find women attractive, soft, beautiful, but when I say something like this, I am immediately labeled as dirty. But I am not a dirty man. Yet, if they find out what sites I have looked at . . . I did not know everything can be traced. I only learned about this last week. I tried to get the doctor to agree that I can spend a little time at home, but he says that would be ir-responsible. Of course, I have not explained my reason, for if I did, the man might think . . . Perhaps he will even refuse to operate. But now it keeps me awake. Suppose I die on the operating table and they open my computer. I am deadly ashamed. But you may say, what does it matter, when you are already dead?"

"I am not saying that," was my reply. "It does matter, for it keeps you awake. You feel naked and vulnerable. I assume you feel totally unsafe. What needs to happen so that you can go to the operation without worries?"

He had a sad look on his face. "I do not know; I have racked my brain. Last night I even went and got my coat to walk home. I have my keys in my drawer so I can get in. My wife always sleeps soundly. She would not wake up if I grabbed that computer and threw it in the canal in front of our house. I thought: after that I will get back to the hospital and back into bed. Nobody would find out. I was already downstairs, but I ran out of breath. I could not do it."

"Don't you have a friend or brother . . . ?" I said. He shook his head. "My best friend died last year. We understood each other. We knew each other ever since we were in elementary school together. We were no 'dirty' men, but we always fell in love with the same kind of girls. We liked beautiful things and sweet attractive women. He married someone like this. That was not something dirty, absolutely not."

I believed what he told me. What a danger he was in. He was more worried about the warning of George Orwell than about God: *Big Brother is watching you!* Orwell's novel *1984* deals with a terrible system in which nothing remains hidden and nothing is ever forgotten. "I can explain it to God," my patient said, "but not to people."

And yes, I too believe that God is more understanding and merciful than people and systems. "I suggest that you write a last will," I said. "In this you state that, if something happens to you, I will inherit your computer. I promise that, if you do not survive your surgery, I will go and collect your computer and will immediately destroy it. I have a friend who knows how to do that. As a chaplain I must keep our conversation confidential."

This is what we agreed, on paper with signatures.

We are safer with God, who knows us as we are, than we are with other people. And I am quite willing to be God's accomplice.

REFLECTION

In this reflection we are dealing with at least two themes: first, the theme of the last judgment, and, second, the theme of desire, sexuality, loneliness, and shame.

Judgment

The thought of a final judgment is an essential part of the Christian faith. God will judge the history and the deeds of human beings. This is supported by a wealth of biblical data. The Gospels tell us that Jesus himself expected this: a decisive moment when, at the end of time, the Son of Man appears. We find the same expectation in the Pauline letters, in the letter to the Hebrews, and, of course, in the last book in Bible book, the Revelation of St. John. So the last judgment has been given a definite place in the doctrine of the church.[1] In our time the emphasis on a final judgment before God's throne, after this life has ended, has become less pronounced in church and theology, even though in many places it has not disappeared.

---

1. Van der Kooi and Van den Brink, *Christian Dogmatics,* 743–45.

Yet, fear of the reality of judgment is still with us. The emphasis has shifted from a judgment *after* this life to our *present* life as the place where the iron is struck; God's judgment is now executed in the here and now. Twentieth-century theologians like Karl Barth, Rudolf Bultmann, and Paul Althaus led this reinterpretation. God's judgment *is* decisive, but it does not take place in a distant future but now. Admittedly, these theologians were able to appeal to the Gospel of John, where the judgment is indeed spoken of as something that occurs in the present. These come the moments when, to our dismay, we discover that making a choice is unavoidable, that we have to choose between good and evil, fear and trust, and take the consequences of that choice. In theological terms, the final things, or the "eschaton," do not refer to something future, after death, but rather to an existential moment in today's reality. All of a sudden we find ourselves in a situation where we *have* to choose, whatever the ambiguities with which we are confronted. In this context sin may be described as our unwillingness to face up to this situation. We'd rather escape, or let ourselves be anaesthetized by the noise, put on headphones to seal ourselves off from our immediate environment.

Yet this shift in what is said from the pulpits only partially reflects what many people think and believe. As is clear from this conversation: the fear that we will at some final stage be held accountable may have diminished, but it has not completely gone. And the question remains whether a diminished emphasis on a judgment in the after-life has brought much relief. As Charles Taylor puts it: a shift has occurred within our whole worldview from transcendence to immanence—in other words, towards an attitude of living in a world without God. If God, who once as the supreme Lord judges humanity and the world, has been subsumed in this life, now we, like the man in this story, fear the judgment of people: he is afraid his wife and his son will discover which internet sites he has visited. He has recently learned that everything on his hard drive can be traced. Thus the irony: while many churches and theologians no longer use threatening language or speak and preach about a final judgment, that role has been taken over by the reality of the internet, the big IT companies and their systems, where all movements and actions in the ether can, in principle, be traced.

Big Brother is watching you all the time, forever and ever! And ever.

Google as god

What is it we read in the Bible again? In Revelation we read about a Book of Life in which the names of all who belong to Christ are registered.[2] It has often been inferred that this means there must also be something like a Book of the Lost, of all those from whom God has withheld his grace. This was implied in the doctrine of double predestination. Remarkably, the Bible remains totally silent about any such a book; yet, it seems that in our day and age the internet has assumed just that role. Google is the new dangerous god. Everything is remembered, nothing is lost in the depths of the sea, everything can be traced. Nothing that we do on the internet, nothing that might cause guilt and shame, is hidden or deleted. The memory of search engines is enormous and limitless. Even when damaged by fire or water, much of what is saved on a hard disk can still be recovered.

What does the chaplain do? It would not help if, when confronted with the fear of being discovered, she would immediately come out with some condoning remarks: "What you did is not so terrible," or "Don't worry, everybody does it." And, in fact, this is not the man's question: he believes he may be able to explain to God why he enjoys looking at nudity and is so fascinated by it. The point at issue is how we deal with questions of guilt, shame, and judgment. In this case it is the shame: What will people say? Shame is a typically human phenomenon, since it is reflexive. I am able to look at myself, to evaluate myself. I disappoint others and myself; my self-image enters into the equation. We see ourselves through the eyes of others and fear their judgment. We fear this judgment because we have already submitted ourselves to this judgment. The Bible story of the fall (Gen 3) tell us that the first humans felt ashamed as soon as they learned about good and evil. They enter the land of ambiguity and vulnerability and as a result become insecure in their relationship with each other and with God. Even before God has spoken, they look at themselves and each other, and then hide like a deer that seeks cover.

Strangely enough: God's judgment functions in this encounter in a positive manner. God's eyes are to be preferred over those of human beings. It seems as if the patient in the story has grasped something of the God of the Bible. It sounds like the words of David who, when given the choice, also preferred to fall into God's hands rather than those of the people.[3] The

2. Revelation 3:5 and 20:12.

3. 2 Samuel 24:14: "Then David said to Gad, 'I am in great distress; let us fall into the

chaplain goes for the practical approach. She is prepared to take care of the computer should something go wrong during the operation. There is no judgment; the patient can submit to the surgery. And can handle it.

Desire, body, beauty, and sexuality

The second theme that is on the table is that of desire, the body, beauty, and sexuality. Let us be clear from the outset that this involves a complex theme, combining many aspects that defy any easy direction or answer. Within the limitations of this chapter we can say just a few things.

First, we have the new possibilities of technology. The internet and new media are marvelous and seem almost infinite. At the same time they bombard us with information and choices. It takes only two mouse clicks to bring us to sites we do not want to visit and yet are drawn to. In this story it apparently has to do with visits to adult sites or looking at nude pictures. They appeal to our desires, elicit curiosity, and awaken lust. How do we react to these things in the church, in theology, in our society? Do we avoid the topic or trivialize it? When it comes to sexuality and nudity Christianity and the church—rightly or wrongly—have a poor reputation. Many, particularly those of the older generation, remember this as a domain of forbidden things. Premarital sex, looking at other women (or men!) brought up much insecurity, fear, and big taboos. Also much frustration and loneliness, particularly inside marriage and, we are told, especially for men.

This statement does not rest on vague suppositions but on the experience of many years and many conversations. On the surface it may appear that today we have a lot more freedom, but the lack of, and hunger for, sexual contact and intimacy have not decreased. The mainline Protestant churches in Europe have distanced themselves from many of the old prohibitions, but this has not solved all the old questions, uncertainties, and problems. In the US the issue of (homo)sexual relations has become a red flag over which churches argue and split. Many mainline churches, among them the Episcopal Church and the Presbyterian Church (USA), have opted for this humanizing line as well in their official statements and publications. That is, sexuality has been recognized as something that is part of our being human, or rather: our sex and gender belong to our humanness. It is part of our creatureliness. Desire is part of the package. Desire for what? For the

---

hand of the Lord, for his mercy is great; but let me not fall into human hands.'"

other as a partner, for fulfillment, satisfaction, for beauty, wholeness, and enrichment. But also for God?

Yes, also for God. This desire in us, this struggle at all levels, is something to be appreciated, however awkward it might sometimes be. It helps us realize that, seen from a theological angle, all desire finds its origin with God. The British theologian Sarah Coakley has elaborated upon the notions she found in the church fathers and came to base her entire theology on this thought.[4] In the eternal life of the triune God we find a dynamic of desire, of response and fulfillment. He is the eternally rich God, from whom all things receive their luster. Our entire creaturely existence reflects in its needs and structure the fundamental trait of searching for fulfillment and happiness, for being seen and known. The goal of human existence is happiness and joy. The pursuit of happiness is a propelling force that must, in the first instance, be valued as something positive. This is the opposite of what Sigmund Freud argued. Longing and desire are not primarily rooted in human sexuality but derive from God. Human longing and desire reflect the divine. Things only begin to go wrong when this desire changes into a lust for power that wants to possess its object of desire at any cost. When one person reduces the other to a mere instrument of his own happiness and satisfaction, and the other person is not respected in her own right. In that case an important element of this fulfillment is lost, namely, the uniqueness of the other who may never be seen as simply a means to my enjoyment. Instead, I must focus on the other in order to make the other flourish. But this can never be forced, as love tells us. Love provides the courage to leave our own shell and approach the other as the other, with the risk of rejection. Love accepts that risk. Joy and fulfillment are *given*, they are a gift that cannot be *demanded*. We point to the distinction Augustine made between using and enjoying. Using (*uti*) means that the object is instrumentalized and worn out as it is being used. Enjoying (*frui*) takes pleasure in the other because of the other.

The next question is how this happiness and joy may be acquired, or rather, be given. Should we grab everything that comes within the reach of our hands and eyes? No, the desire must also be streamlined and guided. This implies discipline but first and foremost recognition. In the encounter with the man facing surgery, the chaplain begins with recognition. She recognizes this man's desires, his emotions when confronted with nudity; she refrains from any nosy questions regarding details. She recognizes that his

4. Coakley, *God, Sexuality and the Self*, 308–36.

desire for and appreciation of beauty (about which she does not comment any further) do not coincide with what is dirty and bad. The fact that she does this as a woman is significant. A woman confirms that he does not become a dirty man by appreciating nudity. This may well give comfort, precisely in his situation of loneliness and fear of rejection. As God, apparently, does not reject him, just so the chaplain does not step between the man and God but mediates safety. This is the transformative moment: the safety and the freedom of the man are not assaulted. Yet, at the same time, the question arises about what can and cannot be discussed between this man and his own wife. It seems that this conversation has halted, perhaps never started, or got stuck on a taboo and fear. Maybe the ambivalence and vulnerability involved were too big, possibly on both sides, and this no doubt had its reasons. And, as we will touch upon elsewhere in our reflection, loneliness in the area of sexuality can get just too big. How much is really discussed by partners within a relationship? Or do we conceal our vulnerability and hide it from the other? It is the greatest gift within a relationship when the words "Here I am" are spoken. Also within a sexual relationship.

Two brackets

In this entire complex of questions Christian principles may provide valuable service. They give a point of departure and a direction. Above we made a connection with the doctrine of God—more precisely, with desire as the propelling, primal force that is not only found in creation but has its source and norm in God. The fulfillment and richness that is in God and became visible in the life of Jesus is the ultimate goal of human existence. Theologically speaking, this brings us to *eschatology*, the doctrine of the last things. Our human relationships, in all their forms and appearances, must be seen and evaluated in that light. The themes of creation and eschatology are the two brackets within which the human desire for happiness and satisfaction must find its place. This means that, on the one hand, not everything is possible, that there are boundaries. It means that human relationships, which are intended to make us fully human, must be trained, exercised, and given space. On the other hand, it also implies the need to discern what is possible and what is better left aside. It may at times mean daring to do something and running a risk. But in the meantime, what gives direction to this encounter from a theological perspective is clear: the awareness that in all our seeking, succeeding, failing, and shame, we find ourselves before God. This God is not a system of right and wrong but has made himself known in the history of Israel and of Jesus Christ as the Father who knows and loves his children and who understands from afar their thoughts, longings, and desires.

Chapter 10

Dave

On Religious Language

DAVE WAS ONLY TEN years old and had been sick since he was three. During these years he, along with his parents and his brothers, had fought against the disease that drained his young body, had bravely undergone chemotherapy, and remained hopeful. Now they had to let him go, or, as I prefer to say, to give him into God's care. One day he had dreamed that he could fly and that he soared to a great height. In the distance he saw a gate. Though he was curious he decided not to fly any further but to return to the earth. He had not yet said his goodbyes.

I had been to see his parents and hoped to catch Dave while he was awake. But he was sleeping. He now slept almost all the time.

I enjoy writing letters. It is an almost forgotten but very worthy skill. So I wrote Dave a letter.

> *Dear Dave,*
>
> *Last evening I came to your home. You probably did not notice because, when I peeked around the corner of your room for a few seconds, you were sound asleep. I saw the Lego car you are working on. I like Legos. It looks like you do, too.*
>
> *Legos are for this side of the frontier between now and later. But I am really not sure. We do not know very much about how things are on the other side. My work might lead me to think a little more about this than other people do. That is why I thought: I'll make sure you get a few stories about what your mother calls "the Land of*

Light." I found these stories in the Bible, the Book of God, who has made everything. I enclose them with this letter.[1]

"Heaven" is another name for that land. But honestly, I like your mother's name for it better. I also like the name "the House of the Father." When we say these words it seems to give us a little bit of a picture of how it might be.

As I said, I do not know precisely what heaven is like. Nobody does, for nobody has come back to tell us about it. Some people say that they have "peeped through the gate" or "over the wall." Perhaps they got a glimpse of how it is. But I don't know for sure.

I believe we can get some information about this Land of Light because God has told us a few things about it in his Book. Not all that much, for as long as we are living, he does not want us to stare too much at what is above. That's what I think, because otherwise he would have told us more. We must never forget how beautiful our present world is and that we must take good care of it. I have learned that loving each other is the most important thing, and also loving the earth. And loving God too, for that is what he likes very much. I have read that he has made us and loves us too.

So, the Bible does not tell us all that much about the Land of Light, and it is not so easy to find good words for it. The Bible therefore prefers to use images and pictures, small paintings as it were, of what we might imagine it is like. In these paintings you see such things as:

A city of peace

A place where lions and lambs play together without hurting each other or being afraid of each other

A place where tears will be wiped away

A place where the trees always bear fruit and where you may eat of them as much as you like

A field with playing children, with benches at the sides for elderly people to watch them and talk together.

It makes me think it is a city where music sounds everywhere from the windows, with barrel organs in the street, for that is what I really like.

Maybe for you it's a city with shops where you can get free boxes of Legos, as many as you need. Or a soccer field, where you will be able to play with your friends for as long as you want and with a strong body.

---

1. I sent him a few Bible stories about promises of peace, justice, goodness, and abundance: Psalm 23, Isaiah 11, Zechariah 8, John 10, and Revelation, as retold especially for children.

I believe that these pictures from the Bible mean that we can be sure that it will be great to be with God.

And that God, who has made you, who is with you here, and who is also the Father of Jesus, will go together with you to the gate and will open the door for you and will say: "Welcome, Dave. Here you are. I've been waiting for you. I love you."

I have a hard time understanding everything, but that is not very important. It is much more important that I can trust this.

He will also care for your father and mother and your brothers. He does that, for instance, by sending his angels.

Don't be mistaken: I have learned that most angels are of flesh and blood. You have seen them. Your aunt, who comes to cook for you every Friday, is one of them. Your neighbor, who comes every Monday to take a walk with your father, is another. And your grandma: I saw how she kissed your mother. The children in your class, who sent you all those drawings. Your teacher who helped you all year long with your language lessons. They all brought love. God has invented love, and what else could angels be than messengers of love?

I say to you, come home safely, Dave. Go with God and he will be with you.

Margriet

REFLECTION

Letters

Writing letters is a noble skill that is well worth practicing. In a letter the absent author is present. A letter is a form of pastoral care, a very special one: though absent the author comes very nearby. A carefully crafted letter may change the day or the night of the recipient. In contrast to a telephone call a letter always arrives at an opportune moment: the receiver can read the letter at any time she finds expedient, even during the night. There is also an advantage for the writer: when you sit down to write a letter you can consider just how you want to say certain things. A carefully written letter is focused on the receiver, in contrast to most e-mails, which are usually sender-centered or -directed.

It is quite significant that a large part of the New Testament consists of letters. Paul wrote his letters to people he had met and could not revisit in the near future. Sometimes he wrote from prison. Centuries later these letters are still being translated and read. The same applies to the prison letters of Dietrich Bonhoeffer or to Martin Luther King Jr.'s *Letter from Birmingham Jail.*[2]

Images of hope

Theology is not just for the sake of adults but also tries to provide children with words and images. Perhaps *especially* children, since that forces us to limit ourselves to what is most essential. The chaplain's letter to Dave shows that we may also say to children what in a theologically responsible way may be said to adults. This letter concretizes Christian hope for a seriously sick child who has only a short time to live. In this case the work of the chaplain differs from that of a pastoral visit, but the two do not have to be played off against each other.

The key words above are "theologically responsible." Are Legos only for the here and now? Or might we extrapolate and imagine heaven as a place where there are Legos, albeit of a special kind? Might Legos serve as an image of the good things that have been promised to us? In other words, what kind of paintings do we make to portray eternity, and how defensible is this practice?

Continuity

The chaplain is somewhat ambivalent: she gives a yes and a no. She begins by saying that we do not know much about the other side. But further on she encourages Dave to imagine heaven as a place with shops where you can get an unlimited supply of free boxes of Legos, "'as many as you want.'" This reticence, this yes and no, or perhaps first yes and then no, corresponds with what we find when dogmatics reflects on eternal life. We are limited in that we have no other visual materials at our disposal than things from our present world. However, the same limitation applies to all our theological language about God. We must use language derived from our experiences on this earth to talk about things that go far beyond it. Is this impossible or just strange? The Bible shows us the way. We should take the richness of images in both the Old and the New Testament as encouragement. Take for instance how Isaiah 26 pictures the climax of all things as an enormous

2. Bonhoeffer, *Letters and Papers*; King, *Letter from Birmingham Jail.*

banquet for all peoples, or take the last book of the Bible in which the New Jerusalem is depicted as a garden city in which trees bear fruit twelve times a year. Such images suggest *continuity* between here and there, now and then. We may speak about eternal life as a form of continuity with what we now know. We find a very radical example of this in the apostle Paul's well-known chapter about love. Faith, hope, and love are different ways in which we may be connected with God. Yet there is a difference between those three ways or *modes*. There comes a time when faith and hope will be no more but love will remain. The same love that we may experience, even today, in flashes and moments, from God and from other people— that love remains a reality that connects the temporal with the eternal. In other words: when Paul speaks of love, it is not an image or a metaphor but something to be taken literally. When we think about this and let it sink in, it takes our breath away. In love we experience what in eternity will fill our existence with full glory.[3]

Systematic theology discusses the problem of the adequacy of religious language under the doctrine of analogy. What entitles us to use particular images and metaphors? The early church strongly emphasized that our human language is inadequate and that we ought to add a negation to any qualification we derive from our earthly reality because with God we are faced with infinity and incomprehensibility. This approach is often referred to as the *apophatic* tradition. It stands in contrast with the affirming use of language, *kataphasis*. Building on the work of Karl Barth and Paul Ricoeur we opt for the position that the language of faith does indeed express truth: in revelation we are confronted with God's coming into our world. He enlists our world and its language into his service. There remains, of course, a distance between divine reality and what we can say, but our language is nonetheless adequate and reliable. For pastoral encounters, for prayer and for preaching, this means that the pastor may use traditional language and familiar images with confidence. In the prayer for enlightenment by the Holy Spirit we pray for the guiding influence of God's Spirit. At the same time we are *praying*, which implies a critical distance with regard to what human language can do. For, ultimately, it is God himself who must speak.

---

3. Van der Kooi and Van den Brink, *Christian Dogmatics*, 756–57.

Discontinuity

Besides continuity there is *discontinuity*. We can at most catch a glimpse of what eternal life, glorification, and fulfillment will be. It will differ from what we can now imagine. Here the concept of glorification can help us out.

An important, ever-recurring question becomes particularly acute around the death of a child: What does glorification mean? Does it mean that a life which has ended too early will find its complete fulfillment under the horizon of God's love? Will those among us who are plagued by a handicap be delivered from this burden in eternity, and will a person with Down Syndrome no longer have that in God's eternity? What will be the age of a child who has died? Do we, in expressing such expectations, simply built on a culture of health and vitality that mainly reflects our present ideals? Or does glorification, participating in God's glory, mean that our entire life will be purified and will shine in a way we cannot know yet?

The paradigm for what glorification means is clarified in the Gospels' accounts of encounters with the risen Lord. He appears among the disciples in time and space and thus he relates to our earthly reality. Yet, at the same time, he appears to be exempt from the limitations of time and space. When Mary meets Christ at the open tomb and the risen Lord calls her by name, there occurs both a seeing and a not-seeing. In his appearance to Thomas, the Risen One's identity is that of the person the disciples saw being crucified. In short, after his resurrection Jesus acts in our time and space on the basis of a new reality, the eschatological reality of God. Again, this means both continuity and discontinuity. Paul formulated their convergence powerfully in 1 Corinthians 15:42–45:

> What is sown is perishable, what is raised is imperishable. It is sown in dishonor, it is raised in glory. It is sown in weakness, it is raised in power. It is sown a physical body, it is raised a spiritual body. If there is a physical body, there is also a spiritual body. Thus it is written, "The first man, Adam, became a living being"; the last Adam became a life-giving spirit.

Glory

So perhaps the best image we can use is that of glory. Our entire life of the present will be purified under the love of God and will shine in glory. At unexpected moments we sometimes already get a foretaste of this to relish. A daughter who radiates happiness on her wedding day, a woman who lovingly looks at her husband, a hymn we sing together, a small boy who enjoys his pizza in utter concentration.

But we must also conclude from these examples that it is important to be selective in which images we use. Not everything is right and fitting. In general, we might say that our norm or determinative criterion should come from what the Christian church has received in the history of the glorification of Jesus Christ. This story is the ground for the church's hope and expectations. Yet it also gives rise to awkward questions. How, for instance, do we respond to the frequently-asked question of whether we will meet our loved ones again after death? C. S. Lewis even wonders about having sex in the hereafter and feels he has good reasons to consider this a distinct possibility.[4] And how are we to conceive of such a wonderfully fulfilled world with so many people on our planet?

Such questions are, of course, not dealt with in the letter to Dave. There the focus shifts toward God as the one who is to be trusted and who cares for the living and the dead. In so doing we are pointed toward the deepest content of our faith tradition, namely, that God is the Living God who is faithful to his creation and who guarantees our safety. On the basis of this faith in the God of life and resurrection, a circle of expectation and trust may be drawn within which human images about that future communion have their place.

4. Lewis, "Intercourse on the Afterlife," 201–03. See Van der Kooi and Van den Brink, *Christian Dogmatics*, 284–87.

Chapter 11

On Prophecy, True and False

"WHAT IS HAPPENING HERE?" I am worried as I face the couple in the private room in our internal medicine ward. They look at each other like two birds huddling together, the man in bed and his wife in a chair at the window. Sadness hangs in the air. The man is incurably ill. Just a few days ago they were full of hope, making plans for a trip in the spring, thinking that they would still have some time together. But after consulting with their oncologist and in a conversation they had requested with me, they had opted for limited treatment in order to make the time they had left as good as possible. "There are a few things we would still like to do, and we want an orderly transfer of our business," they told me. "We are not religious, but there must be something. We have always been good to others. We do not have many friends as happens when you have a business: you know lots of people but you have few friends, for you never have time to spend with others. The children are good to us, but they are busy and do not live nearby. We would like to have us all go on one more vacation, to a resort. It would be nice if you could come to visit us as long we are in the hospital and as long as you do not try to get us to go to church." That is what we had agreed. But now something else had invaded the room. "What has happened?"

They tell me a distant acquaintance had suddenly shown up, someone who thought he could see into the future and who had, without asking, shared some "messages." He had pulled up his full bulky weight and declared: "Bill, sorry, but when I come back on Sunday, you will be dead. I know it when I look at you and I can feel it." Shocked, they told him he was no longer welcome, not now or ever. "But something like that does not just blow over; we have cancelled the resort reservation, just in time. And now we are at our wits' end."

I feel a surge of anger and also pity. I pretend to have a serious cough so that I can compose myself in the hall. "I'll be back in a minute," I say. There is no need to make them even more upset by my inner tantrum.

After returning to the room, I tell the couple that I had to gain control over my shock and anger. "It seems that your acquaintance did not care much about you," I say. "He is totally out of line. He feels free to alarm you and to burden you with predictions you did not ask for. The Bible calls someone like him a false prophet. If you don't mind, I will quote a statement from the Bible that has very ancient credentials: 'The secret things belong to the Lord our God, but the things revealed belong to us and our children forever.'[1] That should do it for today." The sun breaks through the January clouds a little. "Your God says you are right," the man says. He grins: "That gives us a little breathing spell."

Six months later an ambulance brought the man to the beach to fulfill his last wish. Lying on a stretcher, he saw how the sun set "as beautiful as on a picture postcard," his wife said later. She also related that he had said that "with God's help," he had outsmarted his acquaintance.

I remember how years ago I called to invite Theo Zweerman, a devout Roman Catholic philosopher, for a lecture. "I thank you for your invitation, madam," he replied, "but my doctor just let me know that I have to put my house in order. I assume that as a pastor you understand what I mean. I have asked the doctor not to make any predictions about how much time I have left, for that is not up to him but to God. I know what I have to do."

"To put your house in order." This is an expression told to a sick Old Testament king, Hezekiah, that only a few people still know about. It means that, humanly speaking, you only have a short time left to live and that it has been given so that you can bring your life in order. Later I heard how Professor Zweerman did this. He invited the students who came for a last oral exam to choose something from his library. "Where I go I cannot take my books," he had said. "I hope that the books that were dear to me will now also become dear to others. I have my God, that is enough. I am expecting something new."

---

1. Deuteronomy 29:29.

REFLECTION

No double agenda

There are a lot of beliefs, inside the church and out, but not every belief is trustworthy. In this story we are faced with a situation the chaplain experienced as extraordinarily emotional. She knows the couple from earlier occasions. They have distanced themselves from the church and they first suspected that a pastor or chaplain or spiritual counselor would use their troubles to try to talk them back into church. As if it were a promotional campaign by an internet provider or energy company to recruit new customers. That is instrumentalized attention, and we can immediately detect it. There is no real personal interest involved, even though we are addressed by name in the very first sentence. It is attention with a double agenda.

A chaplain or counselor must be prepared for this. He has to decide, who is the central person here? Must the contact be "successful" because that would be in the interest of the visitor? Or is it all about the person who receives the visit? Let's be careful not to claim immediately that "of course" it's all about the person being visited. The chaplain also plays a part and wants to find satisfaction in her work. Our own interest, however well hidden, is never far away. So what in this case does the theological backpack have to provide in terms of tools and directives? We will have to dig deep to discover the relevant area of doctrine, for it is not within easy reach. It looks small but in its smallness has an enormous effect. It is freedom. We find it in the doctrine of creation, in the relationship between Creator and creature, and it returns time and again as a refrain in the doctrine of grace. Christian theology tells us that God created the world out of freedom, not because God needed the world to exist or as a means of self-realization, but in perfect freedom and because giving is in his very nature.

From a theological perspective creation and humanity are neither accidental nor necessary but have resulted from an act of freedom. We might *not* have existed. With this, Christian theology says that God is interested in us. We should always remember this, with our children, our friends, in the local church, in all our engagements with people. The creation story constantly repeats the statement that God saw that the thing created was good: "*tov.*" This expresses something of joy in creation for its own sake. Pure delight, just as when parents are delighted when their baby flips over from its back to its belly for the first time. That is glory, and it is something that also applies to God. Good theology can teach the pastor or spiritual caregiver to stand in the freedom which, we believe, is abundant in God. It is all about that human being, about life, which enables us to give attention to people without any double agenda. This requires a lot from the chaplain, the visitor, or the caregiver, for they carry a boatload of self-interest along. And it gives us some indication of the goal of human life. Christian theology maintains that this goal consists in participating in the fullness of life. This is quite something. We may think of the words of Jesus in John 10:10: "I have come that they may have life in its fullness," or "abundantly." That is the boundary marker that comprises everything.

Prophecy and applying the test

Back to the story and the old acquaintance who suddenly showed up. He thinks he can see into the future and believes he has been given a glimpse behind the curtain. We found this same pretense of a special revelation or prophecy, an insight from higher spheres, earlier with the spiritual healer and so touched on the topic of revelation, private revelations, and privileged insights in that connection. Together with other religions, Christian faith does accept the possibility of revelation, the announcement of something that has been hitherto hidden or not yet known. However, this does not mean that the claims of some superior knowledge should not be put to the test. This testing concerns the content of the message, which in turn often tells something about its source.

In this encounter the distant acquaintance plays the role of the wicked fairy. He announces the man's imminent death, before the next weekend. The family outing to the resort has to be cancelled. The chaplain explodes but makes sure that no one else will see this right away. She withdraws for a moment to compose herself. This is something important to note: emotions and affections tell a story of their own; they are signals from our human spirit that something is happening. From a theological and practical angle emotions and affections are of immense importance. They are part of the *sensorium*, the toolbox we have been given. The chaplain or spiritual counselor will have to react to them in a useful way.

In her reaction and intervention the chaplain applies something that Judaism, Christianity, and Islam have in common: the radical distinction between God and human beings, between Creator and creature. She quotes Deuteronomy 29:29: "The secret things belong to the Lord our God. We and our children must always follow all the words of this law." These words in the Bible set out a basic rule that regulates how we must live with all the unknowns we face. The words arise in the context of the question posed at the end of Deuteronomy: Will the people stick to the Torah and stay on the path of life? Or will they look in all different directions and fall into all sorts of problems? The author of the book Deuteronomy writes from the perspective of exile in Babylon. He knows how things turned out; he is aware of the questions the people in exile have about their future and the threats they face. In that context they are told: Do not start digging for hidden things. You have the Torah, the law; that is the road that leads towards life and not away from it.

This does not diminish the good reasons we have to be serious about the phenomenon of prophecy, that is, a word straight from the Lord. God may decide to use people in certain situations who will speak a word that cannot be directly traced to the speaker's wisdom or understood as an explanation of gospel truth. There may be moments in the lives of people, of church communities or entire societies, when a particular word opens doors and provides direction. At the same time, caution is necessary, since in the past claims of prophecy have often proven to be a gateway towards a lot of nonsense, wishful thinking, and merely personal preferences or traits that had very little to do with the kingdom of God.

Prophecy is not, first of all, a prediction of the sort we see, for instance, in Acts 11:27–30 and Acts 21:10–14, where a certain Agabus foretells a famine. Rather, it is a form of divine speaking in the present, in a particular situation, and is therefore defined by its context. We learn from the Pauline letters that prophecy was an accepted part of the early church's life. We find two examples of such a direct intervention with Peter: in the story of Ananias and Sapphira (Acts 5:1–11), and in the vision in which Peter is told repeatedly and with gentle insistence that the old restrictions in connection with the salvation that had been given to Israel have been removed (Acts 10:9–22). A common characteristic of such a direct divine intervention is that it is salvific. Even in the case of Ananias and Sapphira, who are struck down by a judgment that may seem harsh to us, the integrity of the new community is at stake. In the case of Peter's vision we are dealing with a new step in God's history of salvation—the access of the *goyim*, the gentiles, to the salvation given to Israel—whereas in the case of Agabus the message involved preparations for a famine. An important criterion for testing such direct words from God—one mentioned by Paul himself—is that they must edify, admonish, and encourage (1 Cor 14:3). In our story of the sick man and his acquaintance we look in vain for encouragement and edification, so the conclusion of the testing is immediately obvious.

This is not the place to provide an in-depth treatment of how this testing of what is presented as a "word of God" should take place. We will limit ourselves to two aspects. Words from God do not only concern people or personal matters; they may also involve the course of a church or community. An example is the *Barmen Declaration* which was adopted in 1934 by the Confessing Church in Germany and which proved to be a signal for churches and Christians in Germany and elsewhere not to interpret developments in Nazi Germany as having divine approval. Christ is the norm. And when in 1963 Martin Luther King Jr., at the close of the March on Washington, gave his "I Have a Dream" speech, this was very relevant as a warning that provided direction. It concerned an entire society, and beyond that, the entire world's problem of racism.

In addition, this testing is always a task of the wider Christian community. The person who believes he hears something about another person or the whole community must be prepared to submit it to the community. When a "word of God" is announced to an individual with words as "I have a feeling that God wants me to say this to you," the burden of proof is wrongly put on the shoulders of the one being addressed and individualized in an inappropriate way. Once again: such testing is a matter for the broader community.

Yet another criterion to decide whether a prophet comes from God is that the prophet does not find pleasure in bringing negative tidings. If the prophet lacks compassion, we may assume that something is wrong. See the book of Jonah for a good example!

Bills and coins

At times proper theology must teach us how to focus our attention or to shift it. Sober theologians do not pretend to know everything. In fact, there is a lot we do not know. The horrors of the world, the suffering people have to undergo, the terrible things people do to each other (why does God allow this?), our own future (how many years do I have left?) bring a mountain of questions that may overwhelm us. Good theology differentiates between what we can know and what we cannot, between what we should not even want to know and what we definitely must know. Healthy theology is characterized by some awareness of that difference. "Healthy" in this connection means keeping in mind what we can and should know on the basis of the biblical tradition: God's intention is that we will find life. Or, to use a word that has a prominent place in tradition and theology: the goal is happiness, nothing more and nothing less. An old-fashioned word for this is "blessedness," but that may sound too otherworldly, too ancient, and too vague. If theology is currency, these are big bills. Nonetheless, Christian theology has to do with nothing less than such big words as "happiness," "*beatitudo*," or our beatific vision of God himself, the "*visio beatifica.*" But these are not just words for "later." In essence they go back to the ministry of Jesus himself and to the experiences of the early Christians with him. They may be summarized in a few words: against the power of evil and darkness there is love, grace, and mercy. This capital is mostly paid out in small coins. We do not often see the thousand dollar bills, but there certainly are coins at hand. For instance, when the sick man of our story is taken to the beach and sees the sunset, that is a gift; the earlier words of doom are canceled. God shows us his goodness and grace *en route*, in life itself, in the small coins of our everyday existence.

The meal

The Christian faith community knows a ritual in which that gift is unpacked: the Eucharist, the Lord's Supper, or simply the meal. This is a sacrament laden with promise and assurance. The ritual receives its meaning through the words of promise that are spoken in the language of church tradition as found in the Bible and as given to a pastor or chaplain on the basis of his or her commission. It is crucial that we do not reduce the Eucharist merely to an event of togetherness. It is a meal in which people are assured of God's faithfulness, grace, and mercy by the bread or wine that is placed on the tongue. To put it more powerfully: Christ himself, the living Lord, is the Host, who gives of himself in the sacrament. In the midst of life, in the midst of an existence with so much death and want, the participants receive life—the life that is found in Christ himself. And this happens through signs that cannot be misunderstood; God wants to be our God in just as tangible a way as we physically taste and eat the bread and wine. We realize, again, that these are weighty concepts. Yet, people who come to the Eucharist need not be content with less.

Ars moriendi

Our second story refers to something that has been called the *ars moriendi*: the art of dying. It involves just a short telephone call but a lot is happening. Professor Zweerman shows what this is: to live with the end in mind. This is not a state of hopelessness, nor of having reached the end. He gives his books to students who happen to come by—no stubborn clinging to possessions. Such a generous attitude must be acquired earlier, in the fullness of life, if one is to manifest it when the end is near. The *ars moriendi* is part of the *ars vivendi*, the art of living. The old king who must die is King Hezekiah (2 Kgs 20:1–11; Isa 38:1–8) who is told to put his house in order. To put your house in order carries a sense of sadness, since the limit of one's life has been reached.[2] But the reaction to this limit ought not to be one of despair; rather, an attitude of active response and thankfulness. To prepare is to complete, to make things ready. Human life is lived within the confines of this temporariness as a gift from him who bestows life.

We are here touching on the area of theology that is referred to as eschatology; we are dealing, in particular, with the horizon of our personal life. In turn, eschatology is connected with the doctrine of creation, the end to the beginning. Questions about the value of life are thus at stake in the context of eschatology, and it is important that those who are engaged in pastoral care are aware of their own beliefs on the matter. These steer what is said and what is left unsaid. In this encounter it seems decisive that God is not seen as an extrapolation of human desire or projection, but as the Subject, which makes him the source of hope and expectation. It is a hope that is nurtured by the Bible, which clings to God as the giver of life. If he is the faithful One, this has implications for what lies beyond our mortality.

Clearly, it is of utmost importance that chaplains and counselors be sufficiently aware of their own views. Things will not all be equally clear, but the complexity of our worldviews, theological baggage, and spirituality always plays a role in our professional words and actions.

---

2. We will discuss this further in chapter 13 about anointing the sick.

Chapter 12

Mary, the Mother of the Lord
On the Church

I VISITED AN ELDERLY man who is better at talking than listening. In my experience, this is more common than not in people who have passed their eightieth birthday. The man had been praising himself for his open-mindedness and his literacy. He called himself a Spinozist. When there was a moment for me to butt in, I told him that I had enjoyed reading the last book of the Roman Catholic theologian Eric Borgman. "I am not so keen on Catholics," he replied. "Mary, etc. It is not my cup of tea." I said nothing and then praised him for his garden.

In the Protestant world, Mary usually gets only a small place, in the shadow of her Son. Perhaps that is what she wanted, for during a wedding she told the host: "Do whatever he tells you." And we hear no protest from her when in another incident he rebukes her sharply.[1] Luke writes that, after her experience with the twelve-year old Jesus in the temple, "she treasured everything in her heart."[2] And the whole story starts with her saying just a few words back to the angel Gabriel: "Be it unto me according to thy word."[3]

I had been called to visit a woman who had long ago immigrated from Surinam. She had a small statue of Mary on her nightstand. "It is a pity that

1. John 2:4–5.
2. Luke 2:49–51.
3. Luke 1:38.

they do not allow me to burn a candle," she told me. Ten days after having been admitted to the hospital, she was transferred to a hospice. I went to say goodbye and stood with the staff of the ward around her and her family as a kind of guard of honor to bid her farewell. An aide, about fifty years old, said with a small sigh: "She was at the end of her tether."

We nodded. I said, "Yes, we saw it coming. She herself said something like that yesterday, with other words. She said, 'It's not going well, my heart goes from bad to worse, but I am not afraid, I trust in God. I have done that my entire life and that's what I do now.'"

"Yes," the aide said, "it is nice if you can believe that. No doubt, it gives some comfort."

Later we met in the staff kitchen. I asked, "You said something beautiful about faith and comfort. Tell me, what does that mean for you?"

She hesitated for a moment but suddenly began to talk at length. "I went to a Christian school; my mother was rather religious, but my father was not. They eventually divorced. I was twelve, and I was extremely relieved when he had gone because of all the tension in our home. Every weekend I thought: How will it be, do I stay downstairs or go upstairs? We finally had peace in our home when he was no longer there. I had truly hated him. Now there were just the three of us: my mother, my sister, and I. Every Monday we had to visit him. And as girls we did what we were expected to do; we cleaned his house, made his bed, and did his laundry. I did not like visiting my father, but we had no choice. Fortunately, later on, things got better. When I had children of my own he came to look after them. He was a sweet granddad, much sweeter than he had been as a dad."

"How great that you were able to give each other a new chance and a new place in your life," I said. She nodded. "Yes, it is. But faith does not mean much to me. You know what rings a bell in me? Some children say: in the past I was a soldier, or an Indian. Then I wonder, how do they know that? I find that very special! I do believe that we come back after our death. And sometimes I pray to Mary and ask her if she will let me come back as nurse."

What in the world do I make of that? I wondered. But then her beeper called her away; someone had to be taken somewhere. "Thanks for the talk, I liked it," she called over her shoulder. I was amazed, and not for the first time.

I saw that the woman from Surinam had left her statue of Mary behind. It was still on the nightstand. "I don't live far from the hospice," said the nurse who had cared for her. "I will take it to her. She and I, we both love Mary."

"No one better to take it to her than you, then," was my response.

During a quiet night in the ward the nurse told me she had lost a son. "Just like Mary," I had said. "Exactly," she had replied with a nod. "She is my sister, my keeper; she comforts me and keeps me in the church."

I treasure a beautiful story about Mary that I was told by someone at a church service I had led. He had been present at the funeral service of Aleid Schilder. Aleid was the niece of the eminent, and very conservative, Reformed theologian Klaas Schilder. She had studied psychology, was interested in New Age things, and during the final years of her life had felt drawn to Mary, even considered becoming a Catholic. Her brother Jim traveled around the world and became a journalist, working for a prominent news magazine. Then he felt another calling: in spite of himself he was touched by the faith of the Roman Catholic Church and almost seamlessly was called to be priest at Saint Nicolas Church in Amsterdam, close to the Central Station. He officiated at the funeral service of his sister.

"I imagine Aleid coming to the heavenly gate," he had said. "Peter comes to the gate and asks what Aleid wants. 'I would like to visit with Mary,' she would say. Peter then goes to get Mary. After a short while Mary appears at the gate of heaven and says: 'Aleid! My child! There you are! Come quickly, my Son is expecting you!'"

Just as I thought: Mary is for both Roman Catholics and Protestants.

REFLECTION

Mary

"What in the world do I make of this?" This remark of the chaplain not only sets the tone for what she does but also for this theological reflection. It is noteworthy that in her conversation with these women the chaplain does not intervene and hardly gives any steering. All three of them have an affinity for Mary: the aide in the hospital, the Surinamese woman who entered hospice, and the nurse who brought her her statue. In talking with the first woman the chaplain asks about home, what faith means, and whether it provides support. Not much, it appears. She mostly remembers a difficult situation at home: a father who did not believe, a mother who did, the tension in the house, and the relief when the father left. As so often happens, there are new chances when the generations move on and the father becomes a grandfather. Apparently, he was better in that role than in that of a father.

Faith does not mean much for this woman. But she is somehow convinced that there is an afterlife, some sort of reincarnation. This is rather remarkable from a theological point of view. The figure of God as a benign power does not appeal to her, in contrast with the belief that this life is not all there is and that we will return after death. She hopes to come back as a nurse. That would, she feels, be a step up on the career ladder. She occasionally prays to Mary who is also a part of her symbolic universe. Mary, a woman, seems to be approachable and may be able to deliver the aide's hope. This raises all kinds of theological questions. Is it possible to believe in returning to life without believing in God as the power who brings this about? Or does she think of a universe in which cyclical processes and reincarnation belong to the cohesion and structure of all that exists? And what role does Mary play in this? That remains unarticulated. The hospital aide's case thus presents us with an example of what religious studies nowadays refer to as multi-religiosity, what in the past would have been labeled syncretism. The chaplain does not get into a discussion about it. Apparently, she has no light on the matter so there is no use in starting a discussion about the relationship between her various beliefs.

Moreover, in the reality of life—as in this pastoral encounter—there is usually not enough time to get into all of this. The beeper flashes. A short thank-you; the aide feels she has been heard but off she goes. The statue of Mary is still on the nightstand of the Surinamese woman, forgotten. But it is taken care of. The nurse who has cared for this woman will take it to her. This nurse also feels an affinity with Mary. In an earlier conversation she told the chaplain that she had lost a son. This turns Mary into a person she can identify with, for Mary had suffered the same sorrow. As the *mater dolorosa*, she is recognizable and accessible for women who have lost a child.

This raises theological questions about intermediate beings that might stand between God and humanity. In the Christian faith Jesus Christ is that mediator. God comes to people through him, and in the Bible the glorified Christ also functions as our advocate with God the Father. This in-between position is not so much based on the difference between God and his creation but has to do primarily with salvation and redemption.[4]

---

4. To briefly summarize it in theological language: The incarnation of Christ is not epistemologically motivated. It does not aim at improving our knowledge of God but to

But what does Mary do in this in-between domain? People with a Catholic background are familiar with her; she has an important role in the practice of piety. For many Christ is distant, high above us and near the Father. Mary is Jesus' mother and, therefore, close to her Son. We find a number of texts in the New Testament that indicate that in the earliest Christian churches Mary was regarded as important because she was one of the eyewitnesses of his life, death, and resurrection. Mary therefore acquires her status by being in the slipstream of her Son.

This is also precisely what happened in the development of Christian doctrine. The Roman Catholic Church, in fact, has twice made an official pronouncement on the matter. We call such an official pronouncement a dogma. In 1854 it officially stated that Mary had been "immaculately" conceived, which means that she did not share in original sin through her birth; in 1950 it was added that she had bodily ascended into heaven.[5]

An image of the church

Can Mary have some special meaning for Protestants? Perhaps more so than has often been thought. The Second Vatican Council emphasized that Mary is a symbol of the church. "May it be to me as you have said," she says after the angel has told her about the coming birth of her Son. Mary has the role of the receiver of God's grace. As a woman and as a mother she is specially enlisted in the work that God initiated from heaven for the redemption of the world. She is recruited with all her built-in possibilities. That role may also be acknowledged and given a place within the framework of Protestant theology. Mary is the image of the church. She points to her Son, as in the story of the wedding at Cana in John 2: "Do whatever he tells you to do."

Jim Schilder's story about his sister Aleid is a surprisingly fitting illustration of the role Mary has in pointing to someone else. When Aleid arrives at the heavenly gate, Peter as the keeper of the keys opens it, but Aleid asks for Mary. She feels a closer bond with her. Peter listens to her and calls Mary. Mary knows Aleid, for she knows all the seekers and lonely ones. "Child! Here you are at last!" And she immediately directs her to her Son.

---

bring God's salvation to humanity and the world, and to bring us home.

5. For the connoisseur: The dogma of Mary is dependent on that of Christology. The special state of her Son radiates upon her.

Why is this a "beautiful" story? Because it acknowledges people's search for God and God's search for people. The seeker is neither hindered nor abandoned; the search finds its place within the grand story of God who comes to the world in Christ. Mary provides a clarification and a mild correction. In pointing to someone else she is clear that the seeker must ultimately be with Christ, in whom God's grace has become concrete and in whose cross and resurrection death and hell have received a decisive blow.

Chapter 13

In the Circle of Light
On Anointing the Sick

Rabbi Bunim, one of the leaders of Hasidic Judaism, told this story: "Rabbi Eleazar was traveling by ship from Amsterdam to the Holy Land when a storm threatened to sink their vessel. Before dawn Rabbi Eleazar called his people to the deck, and as the sun appeared he told them to blow the shofar. When they did, the storm subsided. 'But do not think,' Rabbi Bunim added, 'that it was Rabbi Eleazar's intention to save the ship. He was, in fact, sure it would go under, but he wanted, before he died, to fulfill with his people the holy commandment of blowing the shofar. If he had been focused on a miraculous escape, this would not have happened.'"

ANN AND I WERE sitting on the couch in her apartment. Four weeks earlier she had received bad news, the diagnosis of a disease that would kill her. Perhaps another three months, perhaps six, but the disease would take her life. An aggressive therapy might possibly give some respite. It could bring a temporary improvement, but it might also mean loss of quality of life. This strong woman was a doctor of tropical medicine, and until recently she had been active in projects of humanitarian relief in distant parts of the world. She had done her work with passion. She knew what the diagnosis meant. She reviewed her prospects and made a courageous decision: "I have little chance of surviving, just delaying the inevitable; I go for quality of life and will not invest in a treatment that will come at great personal expense. I hope I will have enough time to reassign my tasks and to put my affairs in order. I am not afraid. I will be prepared to meet my God. In the past I have given this little thought. My work was my main focus. If God will give me two good months, I will commit myself to him."

"You are going to put your house in order," I said. It is a biblical phrase that I had to explain to her.

"I will put my house in order," she affirmed. And she did. The people around her looked on with amazement at how she did this. She organized the sale of her furniture, chose a charity for her inheritance, arranged for loved ones to come from far away to say goodbye, and at moments when the pain killers were doing their work, she went through her chests and boxes. What could be thrown away? What must go to relatives, friends? At one moment she told me, "You know, I have one big talent. I know how to receive." And now she was receiving in abundance. Once the threshold was passed, people she had met over a long life came with tokens of love and friendship, the harvest of a life lived in love.

I said, "People say that it is easier to say goodbye with full hands." She nodded.

A little later she said, "I would like to be anointed, just like Joyce." Joyce had died five years before, at age fifty-two, after a long struggle with colon cancer. Half a year before her death she was anointed in the midst of her loved ones. It had been an impressive event, and Ann also wanted, "while she was still strong," as she said, to have such a special gathering. And so we did. I am telling this with her approval, to illustrate how this ritual provides a marvelous chance to understand and receive grace.

"I want a gathering in the church," she said. "And I want to invite sixty people. I've already made the list . . ."

"No," I said—our relationship had become friendship so I could say this—"that is not a good idea. Sixty is far too many. You will have to be selective. First, this is not a casual event; you have to have just those people who understand something of the awe and the holy ground on which we tread. Also, we first need to send your guests a letter to explain why you want this, what it means, and certainly also what it does not mean. They should not feel embarrassed."

And so, on a summer afternoon, we came together, thirty people plus Ann, in her own home. A paschal candle was burning, and there was a large copy of Rembrandt's painting of the Merciful Father.[1] It hangs in my office

---

1. Again, the story is popularly known as "the Prodigal Son," but we prefer this title

at the hospital. The story has accompanied Ann and me all through our relationship. An elder was present as representative of the church, for such sacraments belong to the church. We sang and prayed; music had been put on a CD and to my surprise Ann's guests joined in the singing. A few of them were not used to this, but they joined as best as they could in honor of Ann and the special situation. We read Psalm 139 and James 5. Her two sisters read a letter in which they told Ann and all of us what Ann had meant to them. I offered the prayer of confession: "God, there have been many good things and an abundance of love in this house, not just today, but across Ann's entire life. We realize that we have fallen short of your intentions and that we fall short in our care for one another. We love, but not like you do, and often not at all. We are indifferent and slow at the very moments that count. You are a God who knows this, for you have made us. Forgive us for any barriers that lie between us and others and between us and you."

I anointed Ann's head and hands with oil and blessed her by laying my hands on her. After this everyone came up to Ann and kissed her. Some blessed her, said something to her, thanked her. It was intimate, only destined for her ears; there was music in the background. Then we celebrated the meal of the risen Lord with a beautiful bread baked by one of her friends. When all had received the benediction, we turned to a table full of good food and wine and the room was full of talk and goodness. Thus heaven and earth were connected.

A woman who lived next to her said, "It was beautiful. At first it made me nervous, for I had no idea what to expect. I do not know about these things. I thought: Is she still hoping to get better? Are we all supposed to pray for that? But it was beautiful. Also, that I was able to say something to her; I had wanted to do that all along, but it had seemed so artificial. Now I feel peaceful and calm. We know she is terminally ill, but now it's less scary to talk about it."

Later I heard that, together with three other residents from Ann's apartment complex, this neighbor had invited a church worker to lead a few afternoons of discussion about the meaning of growing older and being mortal.

This is what anointing the sick means: we all get better as a result. We will leave the meaning of this "better" to the freedom of the Lord of the church.

---

which Miroslav Volf and Henri Nouwen have proposed.

REFLECTION

Let's delve a little deeper into a few aspects of this event. First, a few words about choosing to have an anointing. What kind of ritual is it? A second question is about ownership. Who does it belong to? Is just anybody entitled to carry out this ritual or sacrament? A third reflection ties in with the remark of one of Ann's friends who came to the event a little nervous. Is it a form of faith healing? A fourth question involves religious language and images. At the beginning of the story we heard the expression "putting your house in order." It belongs to the chaplain's reservoir of images and expressions and leads to the question what we may expect from people who may have a different lexicon.

1. *Anointing the sick: a broadening of care*

Anointing the sick in the Christian tradition is a special kind of coaching and care. In this story the request to be anointed comes from Ann herself. Years earlier she experienced it in the case of a sick friend. The chaplain agrees. She knows it as sacrament in the Roman Catholic tradition (popularly called "last rites" or "extreme unction") and has herself become familiar with it in the charismatic movement. For some decades anointing has become accepted in a broad range of churches worldwide as a practice that can be used and administered in situations of need. Note that it should no longer be restricted to the end of life. The Second Vatican Council restored that original meaning in the Roman Catholic Church: it was no longer exclusively for the dying but is significant as well for the sick and those around them. In contrast to Protestant churches, Roman Catholics count it as one of their sacraments, but Protestants might call it a meaningful act of the church in the context of word and sacrament. It provides a possibility of giving pastoral care beyond the cognitive and cerebral. It thereby has a place among the liturgical possibilities for worshiping God. Prayer, hymns, church services, and anointing services are not primarily means for us to get better but promote the personal communion with God that makes us truly human. We take our place vis-à-vis our Creator, who then receives the position that is rightly his. It is good for each, all, and everything when we all know our place.

Note the careful preparations in this story. It is important that the focus not be restricted to the circumstances of the individual who is sick and for whom prayer is offered, but that the event be broadened to include others around her and point towards God. Certainly, the life story and the situation of the sick person are important. In the description of the ritual of anointing Ann's personal life story was the topic for a prayer of confession. This gave the opportunity to name what had been good but also things that had been somewhat questionable and those that were definite shortcomings and mistakes. But a further broadening takes place. In accord with the words of James 5:14–16[2] the prayer of confession is not only for the person who receives the anointing but is extended to everyone present: they have all failed to give God his due, as was also true in their relationships with one another. This broadening goes still further. All of us and all our stories are connected with God and have a place in our service to God. The life story of this one individual thus no longer stands by itself but becomes part of a larger dynamic, connected to another pole and is thus drawn into the circle of the light of God's joy. Inside that circle this human life begins to shine in a new way. This broadening is a form of pastoral care.

2. To whom does this anointing ritual belong? On ownership

Our second point, directly related to the previous one, concerns ownership. Who owns the anointing of the sick? As we saw, the ritual derives its origin and content from the broader Catholic tradition and cannot be detached from this tradition and its offices. This basis in a long tradition underscores that we do not invent these rituals ourselves but that they have their ground in a supporting community, the church. This certainly applies to baptism and the Lord's Supper or Eucharist but also to the anointing of the sick. These all belong to what, in our final chapter, we will call the material integrity of the tradition. It is clear that the sacrament is supported by, and finds its origin in, a story. "No ritual without a myth," as our professors taught us. The chaplain has invited the church elder to be present, ensuring that the ritual is not owned by the chaplain or the institution that employs her but by the church.

3. Anointing and faith healing

Ann's friend hesitates about whether to come. Isn't this some kind of faith healing? This association is not so strange. James 5, the passage that is read at the anointing service, makes it explicit: "The prayer offered in faith will

2. "Is anyone among you sick? Let them call the elders of the church to pray over them and anoint them with oil in the name of the Lord. And the prayer offered in faith will make the sick person well; the Lord will raise them up. If they have sinned, they will be forgiven. Therefore confess your sins to each other and pray for each other so that you may be healed. The prayer of a righteous person is powerful and effective."

make the sick person well." And yet, a return to health is not the main issue in the way the church practices the anointing of the sick. Certainly, anointing is not an alternative to medical treatment. Rather, the anointing ritual gives us a liturgical space where the church or its representatives pray for and with the sick person and bring him into the presence of the living God. It is a special form of care. Prayer is offered for and with the person who is sick and suffering, and for God to be near to everyone in the circle around him. It is legitimate to fervently ask God for healing, but in Ann's case this was not done. She was terminally ill, in the final phase, and she herself had not requested prayers for healing. Determining what we shall or must pray for is a matter of prudence, of the person's relationship with God; more precisely, it is a matter of distinguishing the spirits. This cannot be prescribed beforehand.

Here we touch upon a risk that, in fact, seems almost inescapable: the instrumentalization of faith. Instrumentalization takes place when faith, religion, and worship are purely for our own benefit. These no longer serve God but turn God into a tool to serve our own interests. How does it profit *me*? This will not do. The story of Rabbi Eleazar and the shofar illustrates the point perfectly. Liturgy and sacraments must not be instrumentalized and become purely human functions, a way to manipulate God. In anointing a sick person there are instances when it would be fully in order to also pray as well for the relief of suffering, the power to endure, or healing. But let there be no doubt about why we avoid the term "faith healing." In faith healing restoration and healing are the explicit concerns. Our purpose, rather—to use the Dutch versification of Psalm 25:7—is to nurture the practice of "sweet communion" with God and to be open for an unexpected divine intervention.

4. *The reservoir of images and expressions*

Finally, there is the issue of religious language and the reservoir of images that we have at our disposal. The chaplain uses a phrase Ann does not understand: "putting your house in order." She does not know this term, even though, to some extent, she has always been associated with Christian communities. This expression is one of many common sayings and expressions we have that are derived from the world of the Bible. Whatever one may think of it, people in the past were acquainted with Bible stories, as these formed some of the cultural background and heritage for a significant part of the population. "Putting your house in order" comes—as we discussed earlier in chapter 11—from Isaiah 38,[3] where the prophet Isaiah is sent to King Hezekiah with the message that he, the king, will not be restored to health but must prepare to die. "Putting your house in order" means arranging your affairs before you will depart from this life. The chaplain knows this expression and she offers up this image. This raises the question: To what degree should the spiritual caregiver herself have a good stock of stories? What might she expect? Can we also serve people who do not have this reservoir? Should we simply latch on to the life stories of people and use the materials from there?

This last aspect—connecting with the partner in the conversation and with her particular story—is, of course, crucial. In pastoral encounters and spiritual care the particular person or group we are dealing with is central. Their lives and the stories and experiences they carry along are the soil in which pastoral care is received and absorbed. This is *theologically* important. Christian teachings provide the tools that enable us to take with utter seriousness what people already know and are familiar with. This connects back to the universality of God and to the work of the Spirit of God. The living God does not only manifest himself within the confines of the church and conscious faith. The world and life are all God's. He is present outside of pastoral encounters and may have already manifested himself to and be recognized by people whether or not they are conscious of it. This motivates the search for traces of that presence, not just by the chaplain but also by the patient. But searching for such traces is not the only element. Especially when anointing the sick we may appeal to the Old Testament image of the shepherd who cares for his sheep. In John 10 Jesus, as the Good Shepherd, applies this to himself. That is the horizon of all pastoral work.

3. As well in 2 Kings 20:1.

Chapter 14

Everything Must Have a Reason
On a Theology with Holes

EVERYBODY KNOWS: ACCIDENTS ARE just waiting to happen. A few years ago I tripped at the train station and broke my wrist. My arm was badly bruised, too. Lots of people had comments about it, some interesting and some annoying. "Good for you to be on the other side for once!" There was the reprimand: "I think the message is that you must learn that you cannot do everything!" Others kindly started reorganizing my agenda and told me what to cancel. A woman confided that she understood how difficult it must be for me to have been halted by God.

I find it hard to imagine that it was God who gave me a push down the stairs. The problem was simply a stairway that was missing a few tiles, a job for the station's maintenance crew rather than something wrought by a Power on high. Yet, a word from Jeremiah did apply: "Praise be to God, we are still alive!"

These unsolicited tips and criticisms, people offering causes of and reasons for the relatively small mishap I had suffered did upset me. With my arm in a cast—somewhat hidden under a lace sweater—I entered the room of a seriously ill patient that I knew. Every so often she had to come to my hospital for a chemo treatment. She had always kept me somewhat at a distance before, but now she signaled me to enter. When I had taken a seat, she angrily threw her scarf into the corner of the room. "Much too warm," she fulminated, "and for whom would I put it on?"

"Perhaps for yourself," I said.

"Well, in that case, please give it back," she replied. "I will put it on for you." She continued in the same breath: "We were planning to go away for the weekend, a few days at the beach. Once again we have to cancel. I am too sick. This time it is some germ. I suppose I must have deserved it somehow, but I sure don't know why!"

"Is that so?" I asked. "Is it a matter of deserving something? Because of whom or what?"

"Doesn't it have to have a reason? How else would it make sense?" she snarled.

"You tell me," I said. "It seems you have some ideas about this. I will try to listen carefully."

"But I have to explain this stuff to you? Aren't you the one who knows about this kind of thing? You have studied this. I was hoping that you could explain it to me."

"Sorry to disappoint you," I replied. "I cannot read the stars, and if I could, I would not believe what they say."

"That's quite a relief," she responded with a smile. "I'm a little fed up with all those experts too."

"Do you meet many of them?" I asked. "Tell me."

She sighed. "I hear all sorts of things. When you have been sick for so long people just come in and speak up. The neighbor who lives behind me suggested that I must have done something wrong. An acquaintance who believes in reincarnation promises me a better turn in a next life if I am not too defiant. Supposedly there is much I can learn from this, but she didn't say; she had to leave for her happiness workshop. My aunt told me that my situation is not caused by human hands. That's cold comfort, and she can't tell me what good knowing this would do me. My husband thinks it is simply a matter of stupid bad luck. One of my sons thinks I should stop with these chemo treatments. He can't bear to watch it anymore and quarrels about it with his brother. That upsets me most of all. I told him so, and now I am no longer welcome at our granddaughter's birthday party. What a mess!"

"That bothers you, that birthday party, doesn't it?"

"It is always something with that boy. Right now I cannot handle it. No present, no party, and no cake, so be it."

We are silent. I am searching for what seems to lie just below the surface, and wait. I look outside, the weather is gorgeous.

"I am so sorry that you cannot enjoy your weekend at the beach."

"Why did I deserve this?" she says.

"Other people have already told you what they think. But I think it's much more interesting what *you* think. Do you want to talk about it?"

"Dead is dead, I think. Over and done with. But I do believe in God; I got that from my parents. They always went to church, every Sunday. I found it comforting, that there is a God. I still believe it, but I wish that occasionally he would say something. I have always been good to others. I gave others what I could because I don't need much for myself. But I do not experience God being there, and I hear nothing when I sometimes pray. Recently I prayed that we would be able to go away, just to see the sea. Is that asking too much? And then I get this germ as a present. Hello God, is that all you have for me?"

She looked sadly outside, where the sun was shining brightly. We were silent.

"What time is it? My husband's coming at three o'clock."

"That is ten minutes from now. I often see him when he comes to visit you. He seems to never skip a day."

"He is the greatest joy of my life. He does not say very much, but he is always there and he does everything for me."

"There are many questions today that I cannot answer," I said. "I wish I could, but that's how it is. Let me just quote a text from the Psalms: God says, 'For I will command my angels concerning you to guard you in all your ways; they will lift you up in their hands' (91:11). I had to think of this when you told me about your husband, about his loyalty and that he does for you what he can. I believe that most angels are of flesh and blood. Could God's answer be that he gave you this man in your life?"

"An angel—that's indeed what you might call him." She smiled. That is all I get and that is all she gets.

REFLECTION

Explanations

What is happening here? A lot and also very little. There is a lot that's spilling out, an ailing woman who angrily rejects all reactions to her misery. But there is very little space for the chaplain in the conversation, little more than just allowing the anger and grief to flow. What we see most of all is a boatload of very poor implicit theology. We hear various answers to the question of *theodicy*: the question of whether God may be called just considering how he rules the world. We are reminded of Job's friends who first remained silent for a while but then poured out their explanations for the misery that had befallen him. Likewise here. A neighbor suggests that the woman must have made some serious mistake for which her illness is a punishment. An acquaintance who believes in reincarnation regards her situation as a kind of divine pedagogy: suffering is an educational process to which we must submit ourselves. An aunt indirectly points towards God: "This is not done to you by human hands." All these reactions have a few things in common: they try to explain suffering, to put it in a broader framework, and thereby give it meaning.

But could they somehow not be right? Is it out of the question that a solid theology might in final analysis point to God as the One who, in a certain way, allows this misery, however incomprehensible this may be? This is a real possibility. In the Psalms we read such reactions, and the New Testament has a well-known passage, written by Paul, about creation being "in labor." Ours is a world of suffering and opacity, but the apostle insists that God ensures that all things work together for the good of those who love him (Rom 8:28). In any case, all our woman's explainers are too quick in their comments. They are trying to close the gap of uncertainty they see in this desperate woman, but it doesn't work. Not everything that might be said from a theological angle is automatically suitable to be spoken at a given moment. We must distinguish between the conversation God has with us (or we with God) and what might be said theologically. For the latter lies at another level. The first level is the spiritual or existential level, where a pastoral conversation can be useful. The second, theological level is filled with baggage that might be utilized, but with wisdom.[1]

When dealing with that spiritual or existential level—God's conversation with us—we find ourselves on holy ground. We must take off our shoes and put a finger to our lips.

Ariadne's thread

What does the chaplain do? She registers and absorbs the anger of the woman, her regret for the conflict between her two sons, and for what she flippantly said. We note that there are quite a few things the chaplain does *not* react to. She does not start a theological dispute and does not criticize

---

1. The theme of this chapter has been treated well in Bowler, *Everything Happens*.

the woman for her rather indifferent attitude regarding her granddaughter's birthday. The only thread the chaplain picks up is the one that, like Ariadne's,[2] helps her get out of the labyrinth: the role of the husband. He has said that her illness is just bad luck and has thereby refrained from giving some neat explanation. Moreover, he visits her faithfully. This is what the chaplain chooses to use.

The complaint that we do not experience God is widely heard and shared in the Western world. People identify God with something grand, with a sudden intervention, with miracles, with a spectacular display. No wonder this raises complaints: God has been siphoned away from ordinary life. Significantly enough, even in churches the work of the Holy Spirit is associated with powerful manifestations, miracles, experiences of prophetic speaking, or healing. The result is that, from a theological perspective—to use an expression of Marilynne Robinson—the cosmos has shrunk enormously.[3]

The chaplain contrasts this preconception with something else. She points to the woman's husband who never skips a visit. She interprets his faithfulness towards his wife theologically by reminding her of a text in Psalm 91. She asks the patient to see in what is tangible—her husband, on whom she can count every day—something more than the ordinary, namely a sign of the Most High himself.

Holes

In this way the chaplain reminds us of a topic that classical theology has placed under the heading of divine providence, or God's supporting care. This doctrine has received a bad reputation, since in many cases it can hardly be distinguished from fatalism, or (as this woman has been told by some visitors) as a means of explaining away what has happened. The chaplain distances herself from this approach and focuses on another, more biblical, meaning of the term: God will "provide" in our need. "Providence" is suddenly no longer an explanation of everything but becomes something like a "provision," something that meets our needs.

Still, many questions remain unanswered. Why is this bad thing happening to me? Why does God not answer the woman's prayers for healing?

2. In Greek mythology, Ariadne gives her lover Theseus a ball of thread by which he can find his way back out of the labyrinth he had entered to kill the evil Minotaur.

3. Robinson, *Givenness of Things*.

These are commonly asked and legitimate questions, and to them, in the final analysis, Christian theology has no answer—and must not force an answer. This is so at odds with what many people expect Christian doctrine to deliver. They often have the illusion that theology has an answer to every question, and that it offers a neat, cohesive system. But that is not the case. Good theology accepts holes. To put it summarily: good theology does not have a solution for all questions, but it gives enough for us to live with those questions. In this conversation this emerges in a small remark that breaks through the snarling words of the woman: "An angel, that's indeed what you might call him." And then she smiles.

At times we have to be content with a little. But this little bit may sometimes help us to look at things in a different way.

Chapter 15

Lethal Injection

On Autonomy and Finitude

I AM BUILDING A sand castle with our grandson on the sun-drenched beach of the island where we go for our annual vacation. I have taken my mobile miracle tool with me so that I can shoot some vacation pictures. I was determined not to look at any incoming messages, but when the phone rings I decide to answer. It is someone I used to work with, whom I have known for a long time. "Next month my Willem will get euthanasia. It is simply impossible to go on. Are you willing to conduct the funeral? Or are you against this? You are the only person I can think of, and I need you. Of course, we will take your schedule into account. Sorry to spring this on you." I hear a mixture of despair and resignation in her voice. Even at a distance I can imagine what her situation is like. Suddenly I feel cold. And this request does indeed come as a shock. Euthanasia, "assisted death, a good death . . . next month?"

"I'll call you back in a moment," I say. "Let me find a quiet spot." I pick up my stuff and walk towards the dunes.

Some illnesses and situations beg for an end to the bitter final phase of life. I learned this from one of my teachers. Thirty years ago, I wrote the end-of-life protocols and guidelines for our hospital: *"No, unless."* I well remember what prompted us to write that. It was a conversation I overheard in the kitchen of our ward between a third-year and a first-year nurse, both very committed people. They talked about a patient who had suffered a brain infarct, paralyzing her on one side. She was scheduled for rehabilitation but was very depressed. The third-year student asked her colleague: "Have you thought about asking her whether she might consider euthanasia?" I had to intervene. I explained: "Euthanasia is not the kind of thing that a nurse may suggest. Euthanasia," I went on to repeat, "is the act that ends life when the suffering of a patient has become unbearable, hopeless, when the patient is in a terminal state and requests it on her own." Our discussion showed the slippery slope that opens up when we start discussing the possibility of assisted death.

I visited an elderly lady of about ninety in her own home. She was tough and still full of life, although she was becoming more and more frail. Shocked but good-humored as always, she told me that her family doctor has sent a dietician to visit to give her some tips on how to get stronger. "Just imagine," she said. "After we discussed all the details of my diet, she asked me whether I had thought of euthanasia. For a moment I could hardly speak, but then I told her that even though I may at times be tired, I am not tired of life. This pompous, healthy woman in her forties gave me the feeling that old people should be gotten rid of. We are expensive and only cause trouble!"

This elderly lady was able to stick up for herself. But those who still claim that such choices are purely voluntary should think twice. The atmosphere is changing, and we are changing with it.

I was invited to give a presentation at a local church, somewhere in the countryside, about "completed life." To be honest, I have no idea what that term might mean. Of course, I have read what others say about it, but I still find the very concept strange. Some may say, "Well, you didn't have to accept such an invitation." And they may have a point. At the same time, I believe that we who represent the church and have some clear convictions should not just leave such issues to the politicians. And so I stood in front of a meeting room filled with believers who wanted to think through what might be said about "completed" life. I usually start a presentation by asking a question, both to get a sense of my audience and because I find these sessions to be more meaningful when they turn into a discussion. Often my first question is: "What made you decide to put on your coat and come here tonight? What do you expect this evening will give you, and at what point will you feel that it has been worthwhile?" I guessed that the majority of those present were over sixty. A friendly-looking lady in the first row raised her hand. "I'll start," she said. "Our grandson recently asked me something that probably captures why I am here quite well. His other grandmother is at an early stage of Alzheimer's. She and her husband have put it in writing that, when they feel their life is 'completed,' it will be time to end it. My grandson asked me a little while ago whether I would also ask for a shot if I felt I had become too old. I did not know what to say. Can the big questions of life be put on the table and solved in such a simple way, by asking for an injection?"

For weeks I have been chewing on these words. Our son was six when his grandpa died. "Mum, I have many questions, but one is more important than anything else: Why am I actually living?" Asking about, and listening to, the fundamental questions of meaning constitute one of the life tasks that we must exercise in our home environment, but also in our faith communities. For good reason church services in the past were often referred to as religious "exercises." We need training if we want to ensure that we and our children, and all people, do not live in Flatland.

I need this word Flatland to describe the world that I want us and our children—really, all people—to avoid. *Flatland* was a work of science fiction published in 1884 by the English author Edward Abbott.[1] It was a satire on the times, describing a world of only two dimensions. People live in Flatland when they have no words to express what excites them and what terrifies them in life. People in Flatland give birth to children because that is their "right." Flatlanders demand a solution for every problem and want to have someone to blame whenever something unexpected happens or things go wrong. I remember a talk show I saw on Dutch television years ago, about the murder of Molly, a twelve-year old girl from one of our Dutch cities. A few days after her disappearance it was found that she had been murdered by a neighbor, a policeman. He had buried her in his own garden. Various experts were invited to participate in the discussion. At the end of the program the anchorman asked: "But shouldn't the parents have taught the girl not to open the door?" Flatlanders try to organize things in a way that eliminates every risk. They want to identify a culprit: who failed to do what, at the right moment? If all else fails, let's blame the parents for their negligence. After all, someone must be at fault.

I did conduct the funeral service for Willem. I used a psalm, a prayer, and a benediction that I always include when relatives invite me to conduct this service. The day before Willem died I had a long talk with him. It was a difficult conversation. It was obvious, and heartbreaking, that he and his family had been suffering terribly because of his situation; they were

1. Abbott, *Flatland.*

exhausted. Willem said that if God exists, he would have a bone to pick with him. On the other hand, he could not believe that there is no God. He hoped to see his parents and his first wife again. When I asked, later in the conversation, whether God might also have a bone to pick with us, his daughter reacted angrily: father had been the best and the sweetest!

Things that have not been said during a patient's life cannot always be said at his deathbed. I am happy that I do not have to pronounce any judgment. That is the privilege of the Creator, and I have learned that he knows the human heart like no one else, and that he views the boundaries of life and death in a different way than we do. Jesus invited us to address God as our Father. That is not something I would have thought of myself. I simply do what I see as my task: to bury those who want to have a Christian burial.[2] I will not "smuggle" someone into heaven, as an elderly lady once teased me to try in her case. That is not something I am entitled to. But I am always ready to give an answer to anyone who asks me to give the reason for my hope! (1 Pet 3:15).

REFLECTION

These conversations touch upon contemporary issues at a place where dogmatics and ethics overlap. We will focus here on two points: the role of the pastor in a situation where euthanasia has already been decided upon, and the modern value of autonomy.

A work of mercy

The chaplain is requested by an old acquaintance to conduct the funeral service of her husband, whose life will be terminated in a month's time. She is not asked whether the request for euthanasia is legitimate but whether she will lead the service for Willem. The chaplain has agreed to do so out of gospel and theological motives. From of old, the church has viewed burying the dead to be one of the seven works of mercy. Regardless of the dying process, and whatever may have been the arguments for choosing euthanasia, this is no longer relevant if the decision has already been made without

2. Tobit 1:17. "I would give my food to the hungry and my clothing to the naked; and if I saw the dead body of any of my people thrown out behind the wall of Nineveh, I would bury it."

any involvement on the part of the chaplain. What counts in this situation is showing mercy for a human being, a creature of God.

An imperfect world

The conversation with the family had been far from easy. On the one hand they show little faith in God, but on the other hand, there still seems to be some faith left. This is typical of the culture in which we live. Many people picture God as a perfect, almighty, and loving power. But their view is not corrected and sharpened by any real confrontation with the stories of the Bible that show how the interaction between God and human beings often proceeds much less smoothly than we would like. In the Bible God often faces challenges from people who feel hampered by their finitude and all the limitations that entails. Gradually, suspicions arise about the Creator's good intentions. God proves to be disappointing.

In the daughter's reaction the experience of disappointment has grown into a reproach. God is to be blamed for the many things that are wrong and go wrong in life. If God is almighty, if he is loving and just, he surely should be able to provide us with a perfect world. This is why the daughter balks at the chaplain's suggestion that God may have a bone to pick with his creatures. There has never been a better or more loving man than her father! God is to blame for his suffering! We humans are no longer standing before God's judgment seat; God is brought before ours.[3] Human beings confronting God with their questions is something that has happened among all people in all times and places. The book of Job is a supreme example. However, the most prominent thread in the Bible is that the God of Israel is not to be identified with fate. He is the God who wants what is good for Israel, and through Israel for the world. In Jesus, as the son of Israel, a divine bridge to our world had been provided. But the chaplain does not have the opportunity to talk about this. "Things that have not been said during the patient's life cannot always be said at his deathbed." What is possible in healthy days might not be under the stress of serious illness.

This is why the chaplain carefully considers what she may and can—and must—do from a theological perspective. She cannot make up for what should have been said and done during Willem's life. She may not play God by stating that everything will, or will not, be all right in God's judgment.

---

3. God before the tribunal is the penetrating theme of Wiesel, *Trial of God.*

But what she can and *must* do is to testify to the hope that is offered in the gospel and in the coming of Jesus.

Away from Flatland

A second important theme in this story involves human autonomy. The emphasis in discussions today about the end of life and the "completed life" falls very heavily on autonomy. This is also true in the practice of spiritual and pastoral care. Gradually a shift has taken place in some European countries and parts of the United States: from physician-assisted death as a last resort, a "no, unless" position, to one of "yes, in case of." In the Netherlands the criterion of "terminal" for these decisions has disappeared, and the emphasis now falls on what a person himself or herself considers "unbearable." Some states in the US have passed laws that accept physician-assisted death; in other states it remains illegal.

We are here in the middle of an important public debate. Medical progress has resulted in much longer life expectancies for many, and practices of prolonging of human life raise a multitude of questions. What is the value of life, both at its beginning and its end? Who owns or controls it? Are we in charge of our own life and of the life that grows in the womb? Is it not a basic fact of human life that our identities are at least in part determined by our relationships with others and that, therefore, our autonomy is at the very least relational? Life questions involve significant others. And what are we to think of God as the giver of life? This list goes on.

There are many real-life situations where the question of what is "bearable" becomes so acute that black-and-white scenarios are no longer adequate. We live in an imperfect world and Christian theology is quite realistic about this. We humans are not perfect, nor is life, and the possibilities of medical science have added many complications to questions about the end of life. What can still be regarded as "natural" when so much is done to prolong life? In addition, the real questions about death and dying may easily be snowed under, seeing how death in our society has been medicalized.[4] The response of the talk-show host in the chaplain's story shows a sad and painful consequence of these developments. His question suggests that we have full control over our life if we just do the right thing at the right moment. This view can lead to a horrible conclusion, as in the case of Molly. The chaplain has good theological reasons for rejecting this

---

4. Verhey, *Christian Art of Dying*, 24–41.

view. Christian theology is aware of sin, of deficiency, of imperfection, and does not delude us with pictures of a world in which all risks and pain can be avoided.

A second element that the chaplain advances is to address God as the Other. Living with this awareness contrasts with life in Flatland. It is precisely in situations of difficult decisions and dilemmas that people are called to account for themselves, to consult with others, and to bring their thoughts and conclusions before God. We are not in charge. He is the Lord. This gives us the gift of breathing space. It does not mean that therefore all the answers and decisions are clear from the start, but it does open an escape hatch from Flatland. With God as the Other and the bearer of life, we find space for prayer, for care, for hope, and for the sacraments as a physical reminder of to whom we belong.[5]

5. Verhey, *Christian Art of Dying,* 295–332.

Chapter 16

Using the Theological Toolkit
Risk, Discovery, and Responsibility

IN THIS FINAL CHAPTER we want to reflect on the various cases we have treated in this book and the ways in which we have tried to draw some explicit connections between pastoral care and theology. We intentionally place this more theoretical chapter last because we were interested first of all in actual pastoral encounters and the role theology might play in them. But now it is time to reflect more broadly and assess what we did in those cases, and on our own experiences in the process.

We can sum up our conclusions in a few words: for us this project was a risky enterprise as well as a journey of discovery. There is *risk* in tying the domains of the pastorate and systematic theology so explicitly together and to let the reader peek in to see how our disciplines of pastoral psychology, practical theology, and systematic theology interact. Each of these fields has its own integrity and can have some jealous guardians! This has also been a journey of *discovery* since it became ever clearer to us as we went along how large considerations of belief and theology loom in the pastorate and in spiritual care. In designing this book, the field of spiritual care or coaching and the pastoral encounter were always our points of departure.[1] Our main question was: What happens in these encounters? Is justice done

---

1. Later in this chapter we will deal with the differences between the roles of the coach, the pastor, the spiritual care-giver, the spiritual counselor, and the pastoral care-giver. So far we have used these terms interchangeably, but eventually we will indicate which we prefer.

to the people involved? What good do these conversations do for them, and for the chaplain? Following an account of each case came a section of theological reflection. There the key issues addressed include: What role does the pastor's theology play in the conversation? How do theological ideas provide guidance in what is said and done? But also vice-versa: What meaning does a particular encounter have for the theology of the pastor? Does it prompt some revision or rethinking?

To focus on the dynamic interchange between theological content and spiritual care is in itself a risky enterprise. In everyday practice there is a considerable distance between the fields of practical and systematic theology. Quite often we see significant prejudices and lack of knowledge on both sides. Yet we believe that there is an intrinsic and mutually beneficial relationship between these two domains.[2] Often the function of belief and theological conviction remains implicit and hidden in pastoral work. We have tried to make them visible and to deliberately reflect on the ways that actions and convictions are interwoven. We will have succeeded if our examples push you the reader to raise objections or to reflect for yourself on the ways this relationship works.

Risk and discovery are inherent in the very nature of a conversation. A conversation between people may or may not go well; it might get bogged down or it might lead—in the best-case scenario—to greater insight and clarification. Likewise, risk as well as opportunity hold for spiritual and pastoral care-givers because their encounters always involve two parties: one who gives and one who receives, the care-giver and the client. This implies a relationship between unequals in which such factors as dependency, insecurity, sympathy, knowledge, and power may play a determining role. How is this inequality handled, and what does it bring about? To speak of spiritual care as a risky business is not idle chatter.

A third risk arises from the very act of speaking about convictions and faith. What does the pastor say or believe? What convictions does he bring along to the conversation? Are these conveyed, and if so, how? Is there any explicit reflection on those convictions during the encounter? Are theology and belief even necessary in spiritual care? We believe that the answer is "yes." Since spiritual and pastoral care aim primarily at providing guidance on the key questions of life, these practices necessarily harbor theological ideas and convictions. The question then becomes, are we aware of what we carry along in our backpack, of what we have in our toolbox? Or do

2. Kaufman, "From the Outside, Within, or In Between?"

these remain on the subconscious level without serious reflection, perhaps because we want to avoid "dogmatics"? At this point it is good to clearly repeat what we mean by the latter term. Dogmatics is speaking about God, humanity, the world, and their interrelationships in an orderly way. Nothing more and nothing less.[3]

The case studies in this book pivot on the choices that are made in the course of each encounter. Anyone who enters into a serious conversation with people—whether as pastor, chaplain, coach, or visitor—knows that moments inevitably arrive when choices must be made. What do I pursue further, what do I ask, what do I avoid, when do I remain silent? And am I aware that I'm making this choice, and why? Each pastor or counselor will have certain convictions that play a role at this point. This conviction, or our "baggage," does not always come to the surface, just as the repairman who comes to our house to fix something will not immediately empty his entire toolkit. But the repairman knows what is in there and chooses what he needs. Sometimes he may have to get another tool or even improvise one for the occasion. So it is with pastoral and spiritual care. What is important to the pastor or chaplain, the kind of ideas she carries along or her motivating convictions, influence both explicitly and implicitly what is said, when nothing is said, and where the conversation goes.

This is not just true for spiritual care rooted in a particular faith tradition. There are also specific orientations and normative moments in "neutral" guidance that is not anchored in a particular religious tradition or ideology. The choice to remain silent under certain circumstances, not to pursue this path but to facilitate another one, carries significant weight. In most cases spiritual caregivers have no pre-set idea of what may or may not benefit the person they are dealing with. That is why they back off or choose another path when that person is on a road that they see as undesirable or even potentially harmful. Neutrality in such a situation is impossible.

Pastoral care, too, is a journey of discovery. It is not clear from the outset what will be helpful or harmful, but those involved in the encounter have some sense or idea of what might have a positive effect, what might contribute to humanness. Many factors converge and intersect here. Professional skills, knowledge, self-knowledge, and a balanced emotional state are pre-conditions for selecting the most appropriate tool available and for arriving at responsible pastoral-theological decisions.

---

3. See again the various functions of dogmatics outlined in the story of Mr. Çakir in chapter 1.

WHAT IS THE NAME OF OUR FIELD?

What terminology should we use in defining the practices we treat in this book? Should we speak of spiritual care, pastoral care, coaching, or counseling? These terms all refer to providing existential and spiritual guidance for people on their path through life. But each term also carries a specific connotation and presupposes a particular social context. "Coaching" is usually associated with the world of business, "counseling" has a therapeutic association, and "pastoral care" has a link with the church. "Spiritual care" is a broader term but is also rather vague. It is usually defined as a professional activity aimed at providing guidance to people with their questions about meaning in life. It also covers the type of guidance that does not necessarily have a religious basis or any mandate from a sponsoring faith community. One can argue that the practice of coaching includes steering elements that are also used in pastoral conversations. Coaching is not necessarily limited to guiding people from one job to the next. It often intends to go broader and deeper, and in fact does so. One might define coaching as a type of active accompaniment on the path that another person is taking. The coach is alert, tries to ask the right questions, makes suggestions, clarifies things in the client's life situation, and wants to help him to go on. To offer care along the way thus describes the coach but also applies to spiritual care. Yet, the two practices are different in meaning and context. While coaches often work from a psychological orientation or background, spiritual caregivers are engaged in the domain of religion and belief. They give explicit attention to the sources and possibilities of faith traditions. This makes the question of anchoring and having a mandate particularly important. Should the spiritual caregiver ideally work on the basis of a commission from a sponsoring or sending community, and therefore work on behalf of that community? Or not? Is it even possible to be a spiritual caregiver without a mandate? We will return to this question.

PASTORAL CARE

This brings us to the concept of pastoral care. This is a typically Christian term, since it points to the *Pastor Bonus*, or Good Shepherd, from the Bible. The human pastor does try to reflect the care of the Good Shepherd for his sheep. "Care" is the crucial word here. Other languages have a more exact term; in German it is *Seelsorge*, in Dutch *zielzorg*. It designates the kind of care that is concerned with the heart and the soul. It may be that academic psychologists hardly use the word nowadays since they have doubts about the ontological status of the "soul," but we would plead for a return to this concept in pastoral care. "Soul" communicates that a human being is more than a bundle of cognitive abilities, affective reflexes, intentions, and behaviors. Having a soul means that there is a person present in this situation in all her humanity, that she is a unity and a mystery.

Furthermore, in spiritual care—or whatever other label one may attach to this practice—we go in search of what is healthy and strong rather than starting with pathology and problems.[4] Although the unity, power, and mystery present in every person may fall outside of what is empirically verifiable and describable, the existence of these qualities remains one of the principal presuppositions that we employ in pastoral interactions. The partner in the conversation is a human being, a person, a spirit. I may not be able to prove that you are not a robot but rather a full person with a spirit and an inner life. Nonetheless I take this as my point of departure. Otherwise we risk using each other as a means for achieving our own goals.

All this highlights the difficulty of establishing clear-cut demarcations between various domains and of knowing to what extent they might overlap—for instance, in deciding the direction of spiritual care. Spiritual care-givers include chaplains in hospitals, care homes, prisons, and the military. These institutions are all environments in which people face serious pressures that starkly raise questions of meaning, of life and death. No one voluntarily goes to prison, nor do they enter a hospital or nursing home if they do not have to. These places confront us with vulnerability and finitude. A military career is different in being chosen voluntarily, but it comes with unusual risk and danger. Again, we underscore that in all these institutions people experience pressure as a person, spirit, or soul. Despite being vague and broad, then, words like "spirit" and "soul" seem to us to be indispensable. They simply name human beings as irreplaceable persons.

Questions of meaning and of life and death are "slow questions," which it is the special task of the chaplain or spiritual caregiver to help address. She does so from a special medicine cabinet called the "storehouse of tradition." He offers stories, rituals, symbols, and art as possible antidotes to and comforts in a situation of meaninglessness. As the doctor says in Shakespeare's

---

4. The literature of pastoral theology occasionally uses the term "diagnostics," but we do not. It is too redolent of medical jargon. It is better to develop a special terminology that avoids the medicalization of things.

Macbeth (Act 5, Scene 1): "More needs she the divine than the physician." At the same time, "slow questions" do not come to the surface easily; they require real activity on the part of the receiver. Dealing with loss, handicap, grief, and disappointment is hard work and requires time. The soul needs quiet and space. But the vital questions of life do not come up only in situations of loss. Also when things go well, when we experience the joy of a new birth, a wedding, an anniversary, or professional success, it is important to mark and celebrate the occasion in order to give it its rightful place. This too is work that taps inner resources and the search for meaning. Dealing with good fortune takes time and attention. From those moments, finally, we may learn that God's goodness is too abundant to be restricted only to joy and happiness. It penetrates all our needs, throughout our lives. Confusion easily arises when this reality is not understood and addressed.

THE NATURE OF PROFESSIONALISM

What is the nature of professionalism in the "care of souls"—in spiritual care, coaching, and pastoral encounters? Do the conversations reported in this book meet professional criteria? The encounters we present are examples, nothing more; we are not offering a textbook covering the whole field.[5] Rather, we are trying to stimulate further reflection on the specific role, content, and guiding function of theology in spiritual care. Almost all the conversations recorded in this volume took place in the context of a hospital or a psychiatric ward in a mid-sized Dutch city, ensuring a considerable degree of diversity as to the religious or ideological background of the pastoral staff and clients. The chaplain deals with this diversity on the basis of her long experience, education, and personal spirituality.

So what kind of professionalism is involved here? Can the practices of spiritual care be learned as in other professions like law or medicine? Does—or can—spiritual care come with quality guarantees? Let's address the last question first. A medical student who completes her general studies and then specializes in family medicine needs years to acquire knowledge and experience at various locations in a number of specializations. Often more years of study follow, involving clinical work at different medical practices. What about the spiritual caregiver? Nowadays a master's degree in pastoral care can be earned in the course of one or two years on top

5. Some good recent textbooks are Doehring, *Practice of Pastoral Care*, and Mercer and Miller-McLemore, *Conundrums in Practical Theology*.

of a bachelor's degree that does not have to be in theology. A complete theological preparatory education is not required. Seeing that a chaplain in a hospital or prison, but also in a business context, will meet a multitude of worldviews, ideas, and religions, does such a preparation provide an adequate basis for acquiring the social and psychological skills, the conversational techniques, and the degree of hermeneutical awareness that are necessary for dealing with a multiplicity of religious texts and stories? Nor must the caregiver have only sufficient knowledge of what he will confront on the "outside;" it is crucial that he have sufficient self-knowledge and awareness of his own limitations as well. It is just as important to know what you don't know as what you do.

Moreover, this profession is linked especially closely to one's own spirituality, with our ideological or religious orientation as to how we would live, what we do, and how we observe. Spirituality can be honed in real-life situations, in how we experience our own life, but this takes time. In this respect the work of the pastor or the chaplain differs from that of, for example, the car mechanic or the surgeon. We insist that the person who repairs our car or works on our body is qualified for his job, but quality of work can be tested more easily in some professions than in others. Is spiritual care, then, a profession, and is the training for it really adequate? The answer to the first question is yes; to the second, no.

NEUTRAL SPIRITUAL CARE

These considerations also raise the question of whether spiritual care can, in fact, be "neutral." To phrase it differently: What is the distinctive character of "general" spiritual care? Can the neutral spiritual caregiver do more than the pastoral worker who bears a mandate from a church?[6] Isn't it better to stay away from ideological and theological concerns and concentrate on meeting theory-based criteria of professional quality, and on skills for which you can be trained?[7] Wouldn't this help spiritual care gain acceptance

---

6. The remark we heard from a self-confident twenty-three-year old intern, with a bachelor's degree in history—now almost finished with his master's in neutral spiritual care—is a telling illustration. With a smile he said to the experienced hospital chaplain: "You can only provide Christian spiritual care. I can serve all people."

7. As a former administrator at a hospital where I worked asked, "Why can't nurses anoint a patient if you just teach them how to do it?"

as a recognized profession and make it less dependent on church ties, an important plus in the present secular environment?

It is clear what position we take in this book. Professional quality criteria are essential, but they are not sufficient in and of themselves. All spiritual care, of whatever hue, whether independent or sponsored by a faith community, with or without the mandate of a sponsoring religious organization, is informed by convictions regarding human dignity, by certain assumptions as to what is desirable and humane. Whether they draw from a particular tradition or from a mix of different sources, spiritual caregivers carry certain convictions, and from those convictions offer certain answers about the value of life on earth. Their actions and practices imply views about meaning or futility, purpose or purposelessness. Even in the case of an agnostic philosophy of life, or when the personal views of the client form the point of departure, choices are made based on the practitioner's convictions about what is good, true, and noble. An entire conglomeration of professionalism, personal opinions, life experience, and acquired spirituality is, consciously or not, part of the communication that takes place in care-giving encounters.

REFLECTION PERMEATES EVERYTHING

The chaplain in this book does her work from out of the Protestant tradition and a mandate given to her by her church. She is quite conscious and open about this. This means that the reflection in each case study in this book is not just a matter of retrospective interpretation that starts when the systematic theologian chimes in. Rather, theological content and motives are at work during the encounters themselves. That is the basic premise of this book. Any chaplain or spiritual counselor is aware, or at the very least will be aware upon reflection, of where he intentionally held back, posed a question, or intervened during a session. In this context there is not and cannot be any artificial separation between systematic and practical theology. It is a misapprehension to think that practical theology and the empirical sciences operate without normative principles and orienting ideas, that these are the sole domain of systematic theology or dogmatics. The normative principles at work might well be somewhat hidden or more distant; there may well be (although this is not always the case) a longer phase of observation and analysis of what is going on in the case at hand. However, the person of the caregiver plays a role in conducting empirical observations and often brings his own intentions to the process of analyzing them. The systematic theologian, for her part, must ask very precise questions and carefully observe in order to know what the situation demands and what tool from her kit is relevant to the case. The stories and the reflections in our case studies are therefore not strictly separate; it would be unnatural and unrealistic to pull apart what is already interwoven and unfolding in tandem in the actual situation.

Nonetheless, retrospective reflections of the sort in this book may help give further insight into the issues at work in various cases, just as at the end of a game of chess it may be useful to reflect on the moves and the choices that were made and not made. Such a process offers insight that may be useful for the future.

SPIRITUAL CARE AND INTEGRITY

This book is also a risky enterprise because the personality of the chaplain, her opinions, preferences, and aversions, surface—at times, very distinctly. She clearly dislikes the reaction of the funeral director who felt inspired by the appearance of a butterfly on the coffin (chapter 2). She believes that not everything that may *feel* good *is* good but may actually cause harm, putting mourners on the wrong foot and covering death with an attractive dressing. Is such dislike permissible? Does it not violate the integrity of the funeral director? We have not erased this aspect of our case studies or toned it down. Perhaps such instances show that spiritual care cannot be neutral; what we offer up in stories and interpretation is never innocent. Providing guidance to people—whether we call it spiritual care, pastoral care, coaching, counseling, or caring for the soul—always says something, and does something, even if what has been said had no real content. It has an impact on people who are experiencing joy, carrying a heavy burden, or seeking direction in life.

Human life is no picnic, something flat and neutral, and whoever enters the terrain of coaching, counseling, or spiritual care ventures into a place where we are surrounded by the complexity of our spiritual life and inner being, our hopes and anxiety. Things are on edge there. Is my life worth living? Why do I get up in the morning? Is everything fleeting and meaningless, a miserable joke or a bizarre moment of consciousness that we must make the best of before we disappear without a trace? Religions and other belief-systems search for answers to these questions—rather, they *are* an answer. And these answer-packets are never far away, even when we prefer to keep them at a distance and not address them explicitly. They are all on offer in the marketplace of spiritual life and happiness, but—never to be forgotten—they are not the same product. It makes a real difference whether we are dealing with Buddhism, Roman Catholicism, orthodox Protestantism, or an esoteric variety of religion, humanism, or undiluted secularism, or whether someone comes in the name of "neutral" spiritual care with a potpourri of ideas—they all tell different stories with different rituals. It is *not* all one and the same, and the one option is no less tied to particular convictions than the other. This means that the professional field of spiritual and pastoral care is not a peaceful domain where everyone may have their own truth and where the various approaches play with each other on a serene and open plain. On the contrary, this is a terrain with many opposing views, and these should not be suppressed but openly discussed. That is what the integrity and quality of the job demands.

We purposely introduce the concept of integrity at this point. Certainly, the concept refers to personal integrity in the sense that we operate to the best of our knowledge and with the best intentions. But integrity also involves how we relate to the various traditions and religions we encounter. These are coherent entities in themselves, from which we cannot select elements at random. Let us call this "material integrity." Admittedly, many people pick and choose from different traditions and combine these elements in their personal life. We call this "do-it-yourself" religion or being "multi-religious." This mixing and meshing can proceed with much enthusiasm, "feeling good" being the main criterion at work. The result of such a religious patchwork may well meet the criterion of personal integrity. But whether this process passes the bar of material integrity is another question. We believe that at decisive points distinct religious traditions cannot tolerate such a potpourri of contradictory ideas. The spiritual caregiver who knows enough of these different traditions will be aware of this.

The issue of material integrity may, in fact, lead to significant differences in what a spiritual caregiver may be able to offer. Here a comparison between the Christian faith and Buddhism may be useful. Mahayana Buddhism teaches that a human being may become a redeemer, *bodhisatva*, for someone else by attempting to act within the framework of that person's religion and convictions. In other words, a spiritual caregiver from this Buddhist background remains fully within the confines of her own tradition when, in an encounter with a Christian, she prays to Christ. Mahayana

Buddhism allows her to do this. But this is impossible within the context of the Christian faith, and even the suggestion of offering such a prayer would be an affront. It is squarely opposed to what defines the integrity of Judaism, Christianity, and Islam. These religions forbid the use of rituals that are part of another tradition. Rites such as baptism, the Lord's Supper or Eucharist, prayer, anointing the sick, and religious feasts are elements that may not be detached from their embeddedness in a specific tradition. In any case, in these prophetic religions, it could be viewed as disrespectful if, for instance, a Christian would hold a seder meal, or as offensive for a humanist to conduct a Christian service of anointing the sick. That the opposite is true of Mahayan Buddhism shows the salience of theology in interpreting acts of spiritual care.

THE STORIES AND THE GRAND STORY

Are we setting the standards for spiritual care too high? Perhaps. The chaplain in this book remembers how she often had to work up her courage by first cycling a few blocks in the part of Amsterdam where she began her work as hospital chaplain. It takes time to gain experience and confidence. Lots of things play a role: theological education, years of experience in different hospitals, familiarity with the Bible, participation in a Christian community, singing hymns, writing and preaching sermons, conducting church services in different situations, and, finally, one's whole experience of life. The case studies in this volume suggest that the chaplain must be able to draw from a considerable reservoir of stories and images that are part of a coherent religious tradition. From the various encounters recorded here we discern that she understands pastoral care to mean telling people about the Shepherd.[8] This telling does not always include giving explicit reasons for that conviction; rather, it marks how she sees her ties with her tradition and how she understands her mandate. Both are grounded in the belief that the Shepherd exists. She searches for ways to connect people with their stories and experiences, with the story of God, and with the Bible, based on the conviction that these stories have meaning and power that will help bring people to their full development and final destination.

This sort of connection is always present in the primary rituals of the Christian church. In baptism the story of the life of the individual (whether small or big, of what has been and what is still to come) is situated within

8. See e.g., Doehring, *Practice of Pastoral Care*, 65–70.

the grand story of Israel and Jesus Christ. That story places us and the world in the long history of God's dealings with humanity and the world. It is the story of the exodus from slavery and the passage through the Red Sea as a narrow escape. It is the story of the life, death, and resurrection of Jesus Christ and the outpouring of the Spirit of God as decisive moments that frame our lives. It says that history is not yet finished, that God is still at work with us, and that the story of every individual fits somewhere in his grand story.

In our case studies we see attempts to connect personal life stories with this grand story. Or rather: the chaplain offers and suggests such a connection for the individual to accept and reflect on. This may lead to a process reminiscent of Paul Ricoeur's three phases of interpretation: prefiguration, configuration, and refiguration. The people in these case studies have experienced a wide range of things in their lives, both terrible and delightful; their lives manifest a certain *prefiguration*. At some point in the pastoral encounter an image or a story from the Bible may come up which offers a unique coherence of elements and atmosphere, a *configuration*. Subsequently, a person may reflect on his life and experience and come to see it in the light of the gospel story or a particular image. There was more to his life than parents, kind or abusive, and education, rich or poor. An individual's life story is not solely determined by events that strengthened or damaged it. The gospel story presents us with other images, persons, and realities, and a person can find a place, meaning, and purpose for her life in that ongoing history of salvation. This causes a change or shift in our environment and our relationships—a *refiguration*. Needless to say, this is the work of the person on the receiving end of pastoral care; the pastor can only offer, suggest, and point the way. To use theological language: Here we touch upon the unpredictability and freedom which, according to the Gospel of John, has its origin in the Spirit of God. The Spirit is free and gives life; it is a surprising, unbelievable, benevolent power.[9] This lies beyond our professionalism; we cannot organize it but can only allow ourselves to be surprised and grateful when it descends.

Drawing as we do from our own reservoir of experiences and stories raises one final critical question, the issue of inequality between the discussion partners—and thus the question of power. The pastor, chaplain, or coach, with all his professionalism and experience, has a head start.

9. This topic is dealt with in further depth in Van der Kooi, *This Incredibly Benevolent Force.*

Knowledge and experience imply power. Is this bad? Should it be avoided? For many the word "power" sounds negative; it brings up images of violence and injustice. But this association is not always correct. Life is full of situations of inequality in which one person has knowledge, skills, and abilities that the other does not. When things go well, these differences are deployed on behalf of life and *shalom*. This is obvious in the case of the person from IT or the dentist. I do not have the skills to fix my computer or to make my toothache disappear; these experts' superior training come to my aid. What about in pastoral encounters? Our first story, about the conversation with Mr. Çakir, describes a situation full of inequality in knowledge and tradition. Mr. Çakir is a Muslim. He believes that he is the incarnation of Jesus and Mohammed and that he has a messianic mission. The chaplain from her Christian tradition offers him the possibility of reconsidering his task in life. Is that permissible? Or did she cross a boundary?

Even when we argue that knowledge and skills can and must be enlisted in a way that helps a person become a better human being, some questions remain. Opinions differ about human dignity and humaneness. There are deep divisions about what the concept of God means and whether and why human beings should serve him. Practice will show where in this book boundaries might have been crossed, and whether justice has always been done to both the divine and human stories. It is up to the reader to judge.

Acknowledgements

The idea for this book emerged in 2014 after a pair of lectures we offered at Calvin Theological Seminary in Grand Rapids, Michigan. Kees (nickname for Cornelis) gave an introduction to *Christian Dogmatics*, the recently published book that he co-authored with Gijsbert van den Brink. Margriet gave a presentation entitled "Why Should a Chaplain Read Dogmatics?" in which she connected experiences from her work as chaplain with topics in the *Christian Dogmatics*. Various parties encouraged us to pursue this approach further, including Jon Pott, who at the time was the editor-in-chief of Eerdmans Publishing Company, and Michael Welker at the University of Heidelberg, who himself is involved in many interdisciplinary projects. The original Dutch version of this book was published by Boekencentrum in Zoetermeer in 2017. We thank Reinder Bruinsma for the primary translation and James Bratt for refining the text for an American audience. We thank also Nicholas and Claire Wolterstorff for their willingness to write a foreword and for their friendship over the years.

Bibliography

Abbott, Edwin A. *Flatland: A Romance with Many Dimensions*. London: Blackwell, 1884.

Barsotti, Catherine M., and Robert K. Johnston. *Finding God in the Movies: Thirty-Three Films of Reel Faith*. Grand Rapids: Baker, 2004.

Bavinck, Johan H. *The Church between Temple and Mosque: A Study of the Christian Faith and Other Religions*. Grand Rapids: Eerdmans, 1981.

Bernts, T., and J. T. Berghujs. "God in Nederland 1966–2015." Utrecht: Ten Have, 2016.

Bonhoeffer, Dietrich. *Letters and Papers from Prison*. Dietrich Bonhoeffer Works 8. Minneapolis: Fortress, 2009.

Boszormenyi-Nagy, Ivan. *Foundations of Contextual Therapy*. New York: Brunner-Mazel, 1987.

Bowler, Kate. *Everything Happens for a Reason: And Other Lies I Have Loved*. New York: Random House, 2018.

Coakley, Sarah. *God, Sexuality, and the Self: An Essay "On the Trinity."* Cambridge: Cambridge University Press, 2013.

Depoortere, Kristiaan. *Wij zijn van u met al ons kwaad*. Amstertam: Terra-Lannoo, 1984.

Doehring, Carrie. *The Practice of Pastoral Care: A Postmodern Approach*. Louisville: Westminster John Knox, 2006.

Donne, John. *The Complete English Poems*. New York: Penguin, 1991.

The Heidelberg Catechism. 450th Anniversary Edition. Grand Rapids: Faith Alive Christian Resources, 2013.

Hurtado, Larry W. *Destroyer of the Gods: Early Christian Distinctiveness in the Roman World*. Waco, TX: Baylor University Press, 2016.

Kaufman, Stangeland. "From the Outside, Within, or In Between? Normativity at Work in Empirical Practical Theological Research." In *Conundrums in Practical Theology*, edited by Joyce A. Mercer and Bonnie J. Miller-McLemore, 134–62. Leiden: Brill, 2016.

Kellenbach, Katharina von. *The Mark of Cain: Guilt and Denial in the Post-War Lives of Nazi Perpetrators*. Oxford: Oxford University Press, 2013.

Kelsey, David H. *Eccentric Existence: A Theological Anthropology*. 2 volumes. Louisville: Westminster John Knox, 2009.

King, Martin Luther Jr. *Letter from Birmingham Jail*. London: Penguin, 2018.

Lewis, C. S. "Intercourse on the Afterlife." In *The Joyful Christian. 127 Readings*, 201–03. New York: Simon & Schuster, 1996.

———. *The Screwtape Letters*. New York: Simon & Schuster, 1961.

Mercer, Joyce Ann, and Bonnie J. Miller-McLemore, eds. *Conundrums in Practical Theology*. Leiden: Brill, 2016.

Pew Forum. "In U.S., Decline of Christianity Continues at Rapid Pace." October 17, 2019. https://www.pewforum.org/2019/10/17/in-u-s-decline-of-christianity-continues-at-rapid-pace/.

Protestant Reformed Church of America (PRCA). "Form for the Administration of the Lord's Supper." http://www.prca.org/about/official-standards/liturgical-forms/administration-of-the-lord-s-supper.

Robinson, Marilynne. *The Givenness of Things: Essays*. New York: Farrar, Straus, and Giroux, 2016.

Tolkien, J. R. *Tree and Leaf*. London: Allen & Unwin, 1964.

Van der Kooi, Cornelis. *As in a Mirror: John Calvin and Karl Barth on Knowing God. A Diptych*. Leiden: Brill, 2005.

Van der Kooi, Cornelis, and Gijsbert van den Brink. *Christian Dogmatics: An Introduction*. Grand Rapids: Eerdmans, 2017.

———. *This Incredibly Benevolent Force: The Holy Spirit in Reformed Theology and Spirituality*. Grand Rapids: Eerdmans, 2018.

Van der Kooi, Margriet. *Het Kleine Meisje van de Hoop. Nieuwe Gesprekken over God en ons*. Zoetermeer: Boekencentrum, 2016.

———. *Pelgrims en zwervers: Gesprekken over God en ons*. Zoetermeer: Boekencentrum, 2013.

Verhey, Allen. *The Christian Art of Dying: Learning from Jesus*. Grand Rapids: Eerdmans, 2011.

———. *Remembering Jesus: Christian Community, Scripture, and the Moral Life*. Grand Rapids: Eerdmans, 2002.

Wiesel, Elie. *The Trial of God (As It Was Held on February 25, 1649, in Shamgorod)*. New York: Random House, 1979.

Wolterstorff, Nicholas. *Divine Discourse: Philosophical Reflections on the Claim that God Speaks*. Cambridge: Cambridge University Press, 1995.

Author Index

Author Index

Subject Index

CW00341769

Resurrecting Knives
Owner's Manual for the Maverick Poem

VINCENT DE SOUZA studied English and Philosophy at the University of East Anglia. He worked for several years in London as an advertising copywriter. He set up and ran the 1980s experimental London workshop Physical Poets which took as its inspiration the work of Jack Kerouac and the American Beats. His early work was influenced by motorcycle journeys in the UK and abroad, culminating in a ten week ten country European tour from Scandinavia through to southern Europe. His experimental approach to poetry is based on the thought that the American Beat writing cut-up technique leads on to the possibility of what he describes as the cut-in technique. A method in which a break or incision is made after a title, line or stanza to allow for the insertion of different word sections into the body of a poem. So the entire poem is free to consist of a mix of poetry, theory statement, select viewpoint, film scene description, diary entry and other expression in a unit contrasting with the classical purer poem. He co-hosts the poetry and short story reading series *Ride the Word* which is allied to Salt Publishing and Borders bookshop. These events will expand to various other venues in 2009 and beyond.

Also by Vincent De Souza

Weightless Road (Salt, 2007)

Resurrecting Knives

OWNER'S MANUAL FOR THE MAVERICK POEM

VINCENT DE SOUZA

CAMBRIDGE

PUBLISHED BY SALT PUBLISHING
14a High Street, Fulbourn, Cambridge CB21 5DH United Kingdom

© Vincent De Souza, 2009

The right of Vincent De Souza to be identified as the
author of this work has been asserted by him in accordance
with Section 77 of the Copyright, Designs and Patents Act 1988.

This book is in copyright. Subject to statutory exception
and to provisions of relevant collective licensing agreements,
no reproduction of any part may take place without the written
permission of Salt Publishing.

First published 2009

Printed in the UK by the MPG Books Group

Typeset in Swift 9.5 / 13

This book is sold subject to the conditions that it shall not,
by way of trade or otherwise, be lent, re-sold, hired out,
or otherwise circulated without the publisher's prior consent
in any form of binding or cover other than that in which
it is published and without a similar condition including this
condition being imposed on the subsequent purchaser.

ISBN 978 1 84471 500 8 hardback

Salt Publishing Ltd gratefully acknowledges
the financial assistance of Arts Council England

1 3 5 7 9 8 6 4 2

For Rachael, Rebecca and Imogen

Contents

Acknowledgements

Some of the poems in this book first appeared in magazines and anthologies. Thank you editors of *Seam, Fire, Quartz, Terrible Work, Psychopoetica, Krax, Purple Patch, Rustic Rub, Superfluity, New Hope International, Poetry Now, The Bloody Quill, Magma, Poetry Nottingham, Exile, The Swansea Review, The Third Alternative, Terrible Beauty, Poet's England : Norfolk* and *Reactions 2 anthology 2001* (University of East Anglia, Pen & Inc Press).

"People aren't interested in facts, but in ejaculations."
— JACK KEROUAC, journal entry

"Man, the poets down here don't write nothing at all, they sit round and let it all be."
— BRUCE SPRINGSTEEN, *Jungleland*

"Anger is an energy."
— JOHN LYDON, Public Image Limited, *Rise*

"Live in a perpetual great astonishment."
— THEODORE ROETHKE, *On Poetry and Craft*

"There is no choice left but to defend life against the genocidal machine."
— TIMOTHY LEARY

"Go drill your deserts. Go dig your graves. Then fill your mouth with all the money you will save."
— SLIPKNOT, *Psychosocial*

Hotel Dollar Burns : On a Roll,
Jimmy Engages an Axis of Evil

"Absurdly, a poem is rarely evolved into one of
the basic variations of what it can be: incendiary."

Wonder of the nine-storey building ablaze,
stairwells of money-minds steam to a rooftop;
wow, hell reflects on this disaster's mirror.
Known to express, Jimmy tones an anger up,

he hollers his sermon to a high window;
"hey man, has a jacket flown off your back?
Where's your shirt and tie, wad of dollar bills?
(As the crowd looks up, stick man waves hanky.)

Want a miracle chopper to arrive just for you?
You were handed our best rules of imperialist,
hanging gardens desperate damsel in furnace-
hire and fire, one boss on a pedestal set to fry."

Jimmy's eyes glow serene, cremation revenge;
he grins, Big Apple guy falls, splats on stone,
hotel crumbles to a mythical flat-line ground;
Jimmy sucks air, sated by a bellyful of dust.

Accident and Emergency:
Jimmy's Surface Repairs

> *"Positive obsessions of poetry include prophesy,*
> *revelation, testimony and candour."*

INJURY RECORD

The head flung with fair speed
at maybe metal, mesh or stone;
unconscious of a why and how,
as concussed reasons fall away,
the nightclub's late blurring zone
carries into an ambulance's neon.
He wakes to van veering on road,
two medics grin at a maimed face,
smack of taunts, a cruel mockery;
in ward reality his sensors waver,
a wheelchair, memory collisions.

EXAMINE WOUNDS

Above left eye, the shallow trench,
gash split wide to his bared skull;
white and pink strands on grey bone,
congealed blood dries in the hole.
A scab in the shape of a rough fist
pressures an eyelid, closed to a slit,
duct offers its random drip of tears;
socket with samples of dark grit
from crush of lashes on pavement,
a grazed mouth and swollen cheek
tug and bloat a stunned expression.

ASSISTED HEALING

His body lies in the theatre room,
each stitch met with meant silence;
technical moves of skin seamstress:
she sends out a healer's trained smile,
deft fingers dab with sting of swabs.
"I like this guy—he doesn't flinch!",
a needle jabs dermis, subcutaneous;
deeper stuff to fix, apathy and anger,
in church, his crude or empty thought,
as his legs and boots gently shudder,
pain registers, a lame twisted neck.

JACKET REMAINS

Black leather, red line on cream stripe,
it hangs, deflated of chest and limbs;
flecks of dirt-rain on the jacket's back,
collar stress marks from a hurtling night.
Flat out, he leans on an easier left side,
humerus and ulna, an immobilised arm,
numbness rivulet from source on skull;
a reflex, hand slides to shoulder blade,
index finger pokes clavicle and scapula,
he stems tracers of the nerve in spasm,
his jacket's stillness contains no harm.

Jimmy is Well On for Resurrecting Knives

> *"Unidentified writing emerges when the poet abandons stock techniques, artistic trends that steer and constrain him."*

ADDRESS TO THE BOWIE KNIFE

Lines and curves of durable steel, worked
into a tool's nine-inch domineering shape;
weapon of wild killing, hunt and defence,
welded to a hand, your power takes hold,
sharp ridge can peel skin from a carcass.

Your surface is a clue to expanded use,
a notch low on the blade, to strip sinew,
repair ropes and nets, ease stress of blows;
three assassins slain by lunges of Jim Bowie,
a saw-tooth edge to pierce airplane glass.

ROCKERS AND RITUAL GAME OF KNIVES

Bikers live the drag of breakage and repair;
Joey works on Sportster, levers primary chain,
spins flywheel, biceps flex a tattooed snake;
blond Janey dances drunk in black stilletos.
A flick-knife is pulled, Davis gulps whisky . . .

He grins, presses dagger into Janey's cheek.
Harley's chrome shines with flash of blades;
Ricky pulls knife, a unity of black leathers,
red-handled blade flies down into plywood;
Davis aims, strikes nearest to a gang boot.

BOY'S STAB FOR SUMMERTIME BLOOD

The boy is face down on a railway bank,
he's told to drop his pants, remain still;
guy's penis sticks him a weird warmth,
fear inflates the boy into a taught skin bag;
heart pounds crazy on bracken under chest . . .

Now dressed, the child is held by the man;
with a free hand the boy feels his pocket knife,
they meander through woods, the boy dreams
he will jab the knife in ginger freak's neck,
his attacker's face washed in warm blood.

Human Violence Scenes at
One with Animal Innocence:
Bruce Lee in the Hall of Mirrors

"Provocative verse is prone to reject
and ridicule the self-satisfied methods
of the reigning poetry system."

What is it with people in a physical fight?
For many, in its fury it opens some of
the ferocity in them, but most fight
on their take of dominance over weakness;
he fights to finesse, choreographed, a given force,
toying with moves, in readiness for a next assault.

HALL OF MIRRORS I

His feline steps, mirrors times him by ten;
the enemy slashes with a four-bladed claw.
Fabrics in yellow and white, warrior colours;
a sidekick sent out in vertical split reflections.

He slows in the crisis foreground, disregarding,
a diagram of regular combat way in the distance;
his fighting entombs him in a quick constant,
with fear to electrify, bond hatred and wisdom.
He feeds his sharpened sense, a wait resumes,
the eye of energy tamed in a pattern of calm.

HALL OF MIRRORS II

"My demon knows the demon shone back at me,
mirrors give me meaning of how it is I'm seen;"
a fist hits glass, cracks it into fractured webs,
last kick—dead fighter speared on door's spike.

Gunfire from a Mouth of Words
Cuts to *A Fistful of Dollars*

> *"A radical poet seeks to rile and mystify*
> *the priggish poetry pecking order tutored*
> *to marginalize or suppress."*

There's no blame in this thing;
he was fragile from a child,
he grows into his weakness
and dislikes a small part of it;
a safe distance from a doorway
or the sightline of a vicious dog,
some length from the threat of harm,
holed-up in a false imagined safety,
his word gun slips from its holster ...

BAR ROOM OF COFFINS

> *Gunslinger runs hand over smooth coffin:*
> *"not seen anything as dead as this town;"*
> *the bartender pours him a shot glass,*
> *"you don't want to stay in this cemetery."*

The boy-man fires and fires, freely fires,
his mouth shoots into play gunfire smoke,
bullets made of hurtful words he knows;
as the smoke rises, callousness thins,
he has a fair measure of a space
between him and his invented target;
the gun slides back in its holster,
he sours with a memory of his words,
guns himself down, bleeding excess.

SHOWDOWN: ONE AGAINST FOUR

Johnny tips his Stetson, sucks on a smoke,
he tells the coffin maker: "get three ready;"
outside, throws the poncho over his shoulder,
cold-eye stare—he draws, four bandits dead.

Last Act for Lynesse

*"Poetry is fuelled by the energy fields of
disorder, contrariness and scatter-fire dissent."*

LIBERATION SCHEME

It's time that I am gifted a late revenge,
let slow healing seed in a fortunate dream . . .
I kneel on hot ground, this harsh compacted dirt,
a wilderness with walls, the far hills are closing in;
shone here from somewhere, wide tremor of light.
Sky separate from radiance, a bold lifeless blue;
this hand comes down to touch the earth by me,
the blemished skin, my eyes probe into distance,
desert boulders, dust particles line my throat,
in leather armour, soft plates bound to my limbs;
I run compelled, chasing a close imagined prey,
scrub turns into tended grass of a child's oasis.
A man outlined in the shade of a twisted oak;
my nails refine into slim daggers, I fly at him,
I bring buried pain, a fresh yearning to harm.

ASSAULT ON HELLIDMAN

Hellidman without a face, eyes in a liquid haze,
my razor nails streak slices over his bared neck;
he tries to spit force—but his movement has slowed,
with cuts, blood wets the mound of his stained chest;
fallen to ground, he reaches out for pity and lenience,
points a gnarled finger at a creature under the tree;
to finish him, I knife at soft slabs of his outer flesh.
I pile sections of meat—with a pool of clear water
to mirror the face of a twin *Hellidman* accomplice,
his mud-caked hands are encircled around my throat.
Quickly, my fingers thin into coils of sharpened wire;

each rip is made with care, I use skill to maim him,
saw at flesh, muscle and nail—he falls in sludge,
head coated in muddy slime, an ornament of bone,
a signal to cease and make a pyre from all I wear.

DRESSING IN THE MORGUE

In these overalls, I pass through metal doors;
I feel bliss as they pierce and pump into my dolls.
Here in the safest vault, their bodies all I wish for,
these devils I've known are now my props in play;
on steel tables, their stuffing scooped out, replaced
by such tender insides, then stitched back to shape;
I stand by *Hellidman*, a virgin for my paint spray,
I'll guild him in a handsome tone, I can even glint
an intelligent vigour in his actual imbalanced eyes.
On a chair by me are suits for my rigid best men;
I zip comical pants, button shirt on a tidied frame,
under my deft handiwork, the signature of a ghoul;
I brush a fringe of straw hair, now subtly in place,
both of you groomed back to life, a final seduction,
my new romance—your remains are set to move me.

Spoken Bollocks of
Therapists One and Two

"As a lone poet with total independence—you
are free to thrive under the radar, you lose
the false craving for consent."

Therapist one: this middle-aged thing
with dyed ginger hair, chain-store brown
court shoes. She half smiles as she says:
"so each time you are rejected or axed
from a job you are shafted up the arse."

When the client speaks his voice
changes from a man's speech into
the high-pitched venting of a
scared hysterical child . . .

This does and doesn't exist,
down in the point of its dream;
gloom hung in our first history,
the way I grew as your inferior,
could you like yourself for that?

Big theories to my slow learning,
in helpful power of your control;
all my ages light as a missing kiss,
do you know how you transfix me,
pump crisis in a statement stream?

Therapist two: as timid and mousey
as a woman gets. Sensible black lace-up
boots, weeks since they were last polished.
She says: "you're quitting, but you may
need therapy for the rest of your life."

When the client speaks his vocal
chords waver within their band
range, there is no modulation . . .

Gifts from me and gouging by you,
make me all knowing about myself;
such a laugh to spit the basics out,
you tend to stick your oar in bruises,
this seat's for me to be avidly true.

Close in, when my volume gets low,
you read a nature till character sucks;
we can question with untangled arms,
you gawp as my acting staggers out,
a shy performer who says too much.

Examining the Joy
Rider's Dental Record
(Speed is Jimmy's Kick)

*"In the core of the poet's mind is a deep
vein of disturbance and unassailable loss."*

Fired-up at the wheel
of a fuel-injected car,
he is consumed
by his manic driving,
the drunken skill,
a decision to use
the car as a javelin,
its speed as a stone
to pelt at the road
and everything,
even the mounting of fear,
he can defend as addiction.

They walk from the crash
in the vice of elation,
with an idea of renewing lust;
they were used to their sex as
limbs contorted in coupling;
the tactical skins, scented rush,
pass of stimulus and touching;
but now their lips are sponges,
him beating kisses
on her ecstatic gums,
him smashing teeth onto hers,
hissing spit in fierce eroticism.

> *(He sometimes runs a finger,
> examining the edge of a front incisor;
> he finds a nick of broken enamel,
> the blemish once made
> by a demon in his alter ego).*

Jimmy's Class War:
Oxbridge Entrance Exam

His wellspring starts to tap
into angst concentrate . . .

Right, the point of doing this is to
bash down doors to better accents,
class avalanche, ancestry of snobs;
a gold ladder rises from life's plod.
So my crudeness bucks the system,
"sod it!" says my amusement sump.
At a desk, I behave for another test:

1. IN PLATE TECTONICS WHAT
HAPPENS AT A CONSTRUCTIVE
BOUNDARY?

I start to scribble: "When two bits of
underground land scrape together and
then scrape apart, the whole of the land
starts to stress and strain and shudder and
this is not a good thing for the future stability
of the soil on top of it . . . blah, blah, blah. . . ."

Nice, I spend an hour penning shit,
string dumb words in spurious doodle;
gift colleges my text of mental mush.
Clock me, examiner, cringe and lose it;
brainlessness in a character who flops.
I finish with my fattened mad full stop;
dud page implosion, unclassified pass.

Ethics in the Void of Telesales

Sounds like the commentary of a token race
where the horses are all called *Said It Before*;
it's a message repeated by people machines,
as words mash in the bowl of a mouth,
slick talk coated in a smooth saliva.
"I'm wondering" is clearly said
and I am a liar of some conviction.

Honesty crushed by a boa constrictor,
lips in the shape of a moderate boast,
intention spills from a saccharine smile;
fingers peck buttons, front teeth are bared,
an ear is listening to *"can you help me?"*;
linkage in phrases, department of sighs,
speed dialler smirks, then nails his sale.

Painting by Killers

*"Poetry offers the writer a miraculous chance
to unlock your innermost being, assuming
you're bold enough to take it."*

Extreme in the ways of sadists,
this man with a voice in his head
telling him to attack prostitutes,
a mission to find compelling victims;
he obeyed, in skilled and fast assaults,
to make up his own set of carcasses;
each one a blank canvass of struggling,
a range of jerks as he thrust inside them
(some dead, some alive, some part alive),
a screwdriver and toolbox by his side.

He took to his sketchpad in prison,
decided to paint a picture of Jesus;
it's the face that everyone knows,
solemn, in long hair and a beard
and looking out from the portrait,
the core of a ghoul's gleaming eyes.
He had burrowed inside a saviour,
roles swapped as a change of clothing;
did he do this in praise or perversity,
adding his touch, a twist on holiness?

A soft spoken controller of carnage,
shooter from Capote's *In Cold Blood*;
an easy-going man who gunned down
a family of Christians in the Midwest;
he broke into their home, tied them up
in separate rooms and his subjects
all got a shotgun blast in the head;
blood and hair splattered on the walls

(he'd imagined these graphic effects,
his thrill when the acts were planned).

In his final days on death row
he spoke a lot of his life as a boy,
how he'd done this painting of Jesus
(a priest had said it was beautiful)
and as he stepped up to the gallows,
the wardens could sense his bravado;
as he hung there losing his breath
did he accept or curse the cross,
could he relax about the murders,
feel good about his painting of Jesus?

> *Get your brush and paints out*
> *and see what you're made of;*
> *Jack Kerouac ended like this.*
> *When dying of chronic alcoholism*
> *he painted many scenes of the cross*
> *and so did I. When I was ten, I did*
> *the Stations of the Cross at school;*
> *this incredible setter of examples,*
> *crouching, exhausted under wood,*
>
> *thighs thicker than extended arms,*
> *a backdrop of blue and white life,*
> *browns from a swift simplicity;*
> *they could see all my paintings*
> *on the wall of the assembly hall;*
> *I remember the fantasy of thinking*
> *I'd done these great works of art,*
> *even though I'd slapped paint down,*
> *taking very little care of them.*

Contract with the Count

*"An addictive, rollercoaster, primitive love of
an entire language—the propulsion to write poetry,
embrace it as soul mate, mistress, whore."*

Terms and conditions of your use
are written in the failure of you,
the emptiness you give as love.
I am transfixed by longing;
the power you have over me
was exercised in pure form;
you asked me to leave behind
all I am and all I value
and I was quick to obey;
I discarded people in your name

and a sorrow glittered
in their ideal suffering eyes;
my indifference was dramatised,
this was my first real assault
on nostalgia and loyalty;
I left a home and relationship
and became a definite vacancy,
a vessel for you to transfer spirit;
I wasn't much of an entity,
I desired your partisan will.

Lining a Crypt for Love

You change my dream of you;
when I give into your ways
I'm lucky if all I lose
is my balance between
the paralysis of liking you
and staring at a resting place
where I can remain alone.

This is a vital danger;
me losing my personality
to become an echo of you,
so I accept any variant
of your behaviour;
but whoever you are
you can't stop my trust

in the surety of words
or send me to a distance
to work my rage in pictures;
you bind me to your thinking,
though I'll never allow myself
to be grafted on your skin.
I don't have a sense of you,

even if you know where I was
and the unrolling present
in which you help me discern.
I've been preparing for your return;
it's true I am no longer the person
who would abandon my life
to prove I can do your will.

I have further and furious reasons
to protect those close to me;
even so, I'm asking you to wait,
I no longer bow to your autonomy;
reward me now for feeling nothing,
let a pause occur, a chamber open,
seal the fate on our evolving selves.

Exit the Dragon

The best behaviour can lead
to a violent outburst,
as a faithful act
is followed by a lunge
of methodical jaws;
then the measure
of impulsive rage,
flick of fire-breathing tongue.

For example:

When I repeatedly wrong those I love,
it is then I address the nature
of artificial constant good;
my savagery roughens,
my skins become ridiculously soft,
I'm aggressively contrite,
I have the nine lives
of a remorseful child.

Skewed Trinity:
Son, Father, Ghost

First known as the errant child of Satan,
raw skull, ears like arrowheads torched black,
his reptile face slopes to an armoured beak,
he rides mountains by night, bareback;
eyes cry tar into moon and lake,
coiled tail stiffens, aiming at stars.

In battledress of ageing gold, sword raised,
wings stretched in show and a crimson robe;
his voice preaches a knowing sound,
the face a chorus of features in one;
powdered cheeks of clown or vampire,
painted lips in a crazed and solemn smile.

The silent one, master of a moving image,
it sheds a skin, shifts from babe to lizard;
hand becomes a supple claw, limb lashes down,
once Medusa, once a gargoyle hung from the sun,
they say lava sets in its mouth, that sky falls
when it signs a cross, prays in the name of Judas.

Copenhagen Zoo:
Pen for a Polar Bear

Yellowy white giant
with a programme
of forced economy,
action in a muted lair;
master of savagery

with the fierce
hunt and slay rhythm,
stealth placed in a cage;
so this is the beast
of blunted behaviour,

a killer bloodstream
held in abeyance,
jaws with a stunted role:
it swings a muscular neck,
once, twice, three times

to a metronome beat,
then the weighted paws
land in a fixed routine;
it parades on a catwalk
in a frenzy that slows,

it moves with repetition,
sequence and monotony,
energy confined to a den;
the stride cut to steps,
as new endurance evolves.

Coded Breeze

For a while in Italy
the water might as well be wine;
the lake is white-blue
and I watch the windsurfers
as they stretch out, steering the sail;
they criss-cross on the moving surface.
It's all action and colour
and I get the message
in a coded breeze:

> *on the shore*
> *a girl dismantles a sail;*
> *she lifts the cross-frame*
> *onto her shoulder*
> *and struggles up the path,*
> *stumbling once.*

Social Grave

A stack of femurs in an open grave,
a resting place for the travelled legs
of angle walks, arc swims, coital lays,
their skulls the weirdest Toby jugs
with eyeless frowns from fleshy days;
head of baker, leg of cabinet maker,
leg of dullard, head of cream of crop,
head of buxom wench, leg of clever clogs,
left and right footers, slender clubs,
a class of craniums and fossilised loves.

Squawking about Dartmoor

Good place this . . .

Young evolving rug,
wreckage of old
when molten pressure
rose to a welling halt,
then granite reared
in Haytor peak,
map lines bent
on a domed upland;
now streams run,
stone resists,
gorse sucks hard
on the wind;

great slabs lie
on a slope of isolation,
as grey turns blue
in the banner of sky
and people say "this is the life"
as they picnic by the roadside,
a scatter of canned drivers
umbilically joined to cars
(with their own good reasons
they relax as time rolls by)
and the moor gets on
with the job of seasons;

a cycle of relative charm,
give or take some mist or rain
or the weighted eyes of walkers;
there are brief rewards
for some who look below,
at the patchwork
of fields and towns,

a chess board of portioned land,
the incestuous sight
of colours with no joins,
light directed
on a rural stage set . . .

   it's like that.

A Metrical Norfolk

On the church tower
loss rises, anger slips,
human beings cling
like moss to the walls,
voices whirl around
in a mood of fixed opinion,
as their eyes search deeper
down through the fields,
into worm furrows, insect stiles,

while the land drains rain
and greens grow strong
in some distant range
of fells and peaks;
a needlepoint of light
rides on a particle of soil
that leans on a blade of grass,
from the metrics of near to far
a scale appears for Norfolk.

Rock Formation Answers

"Emphatic aims of an experimental poet:
to re-set parameters, unravel staple rules,
pave access to rogue technique."

A rock face carved
in an open sea of years;
shapes of no possible form
pulverized on the edge of order,
a stark shadow stencilled
on a terrace of broad light;
then a flying horseman
with a message for the sand;
a head that hangs down
having said all it's got to say
and fathered some of the answers:

"Things are what they seem."

"It is acceptable not to love someone,
but it is unacceptable not to be loved."

"When you dream too many dreams
the world is not your home."

Sea and Her Emotion

Alone on the end of the pier
with breakers rushing in at me
and willing what comes easy,
because the clouds
are pulling their weight,
a workforce of deflectors
and shields against the sun;
carried by the wind
they block sun from the sky
and shadows like shoals of fish

come rolling by;
the shadows lighten me,
with my turn of thoughts
now splashed in the open;
the sun bursts through again,
sea crashes in a production line
as water's sheen details itself,
a plane of glitter in the light.
That's when my mood saddens,
only because moods sadden.

Walking back along the pier
there are bent fishing rods
pointing like aerials
at Shoreham power station;
I stare at two giant stacks,
two fingers in the air;
the ones fishing know the point
and pointlessness of hard graft;
they sense all you need to do
is wait, then gaze and wonder,

take a lead from the motionless
because there is no limit of time.
Why change your course when
a next event may never happen?
Why cram your mind with rules
or crave freedoms that die away?
The managing director of emotion
is the little girl sitting on the pier
with tattered shoes and
an unpolluted human look;

she knows life is the dream
of waters rippling under the pier,
it's the nature of little girls like her
who laugh at anything they want to,
at goldfish in a tank, at the sea pushing,
then weakening and being unnoticed
or too much in its moving attraction
and held as a symbol of something,
as tide sends bathers into their shells,
the endless waves lap over land's wall.

Always More Definition

*"Images and feelings fused in a rhythmical
transcript, a body of electrified words: styled,
orderly and chaotic."*

This evening is too detailed
to be taken in at once;
sky reds, greys and blues
whirlpool in the stagnant light,
the glow of dusk fans down
like drama at the end of day;
clouds reduce and float away
in telescopic waves,
everything seems hollowed out
and outlined with a razor

and there is a steady count
as a windmill with three blades
clocks the view
in and out of focus
and there is one more pastel wall,
one more landscape of slants,
one more slab of physics
in the parted whole,
in the down and upswing
of always more definition.

Sunset Tang

I the smiler, misery guts. I see it,
the botched colour, residue of day;
I stir when the sun gets all sleepy,
as it mellows, goes for the jugular.

Bluffing about Moraine

Curt and usually moody,
observe me above
as I extend a voice
to say the rarefied,
where words used at you
are doves rounding gulls,
perched on the wonder
of slack phone wires.

On ground level,
I yell as I crumble,
F-word unlucky charms,
classic dustcart nonsense;
I swear I mean opposites,
till the din gets lost
and abuse compacts
in a bluff mantle.

Erode a passage
and there's the tense,
blabbing and its formations,
a volume of drunken hatred,
odds and ends of affection grit;
bedtime's soaked in your vapour,
embraces lay a private spawn,
plus my mouth's moraine.

His Divided Self

He'd lost half the use of his body,
he had half a pair of eyes, half a mouth and so on;
when he was awake he saw whole spiders on the wall,
when he slept his blood slowed in suspended limbs.
At times he was emptied of all breath,
a cheek would burn, a look would tend to implode;

his words were a slurring of clinical requests,
his shouts lengthened to show the arrival of pain.
Women came with tender smiles, tyrannical hearts;
they would pour their love in generous measures,
they would stroke his hands by way of solace
and wipe the tears from both sides of his face.

Ghosting of Her Love

Her replay starts
by retracing him
on the pattern of gravel,
her eyes embracing
sane white lines,
deviant sprawling of skid.

She's cried a night rain's blind of tears,
met morning air as fresh monoxide,
been a phantom hitcher postponing the crash;
she's taken the wheel on a hindsight steer,
drained dare from his scarless neck,
slammed a speedo's eyelash still.

In Uniform

His stories had so little in them,
all I can make out is a boy,
barefoot hunter of animals and birds,
a catapult the range of his hands.

As a man he did loads of snapped salutes,
got them back, wore his shoulder stripes,
the angle of his cap tipped in polite bravado;
award is the accent, military and borrowed.

Retired and casual, now he photographs family;
dishevelled mouths, blinks, legs losing equilibrium.
Drawers bulge with packets of undisciplined shots,
some orderly beauties, exceptions obeying focus.

London Erection

In the daylight
eyes speed at you
like car headlights,
bodies hurtle as if they
belong to somebody else

and now and again
I expect a hand
or an eye or womb
to imagine it's alive
and able to do anything.

I loathe and praise Oxford Street,
I want shops to stock virgin births;
in a thousand paper bag mouths
(my good moist one among them),
a tongue erects and says:

> *"I am the arousal,*
> *the junk, the jackpot,*
> *the refined emptiness,*
> *the smeared layers*
> *of London — its yell of sirens,*
> *the passing rattle of pistons,*
> *the repeating way it is born."*

Getting it from the Mirror

Soho bar people, sliding in a still life,
walkers cross the screen in my head;
full frontal, the illuminated street,
an evolving copy of the same view
kept in motion on the wall mirror.

In ornate gold and virtuously clean,
at an angle of ten degrees to the eye;
each pelvis is dressed, limp arms hang,
a shaft of light points down to shoes,
smoke gets blown on a haze of gender.

Males kiss cheeks, exaggerate embraces;
a drinker with a leg in plaster is flirting,
eyes widen, ovals of an expanding mouth;
most of us stare at the jeep parked outside,
the one in full leathers, easy by the entrance.

Anatomy Show*

She dressed to murder in wired explosives,
she passed him flowers and triggered death:
his blood, tan and guts, his tended nails
combusted in a multifarious scheme;
he the statesman of scattered bits,
he the human who got to reconstruct
as larynx lung, heart ribs, pancreas hips,
or freak fusions that sizzled and bled;
then they reformed the jigsaw corpse,
bone parts to bones, sinew to sinew;
they burnt him on a public pyre,
split the ash into thirty invincible urns;
so he could spread the word still spreading
or be re-assassinated at simultaneous rallies,
spinal ash wanting to drum up votes,
ear-drum ash working on a reduction in tax,
colon ash helping with the candidate's role.

* Written after the assassination of Rajiv Gandhi. He was killed when a woman offering flowers triggered a bomb concealed beneath her dress. His ashes were used on a subsequent party campaign trail.

English Channels

So people are apart.

The girl is an island,
a face with inclusive meanings;
she has too many freckles and curls,
her mouth is slung with emotion;
she's more vivid than people are,
feelings come out of her
like they belong outside,
as if the way she is
has little to do with her.

The man is a pale striated sky;
his grey hair is swept back,
a geology shows in his eyes,
there are landmarks of time,
the years that grain his being;
his cheekbones jut through skin,
his mouth is a familiar valley,
the voice that stays unspoken,
a movement nearing an end.

> *Do they have clashes in common,*
> *a gulf where they both belong?*

Goliath and Goliath and Goliath
(The Battle to Lead a Party)

Disrobing in the red-blue, blue-red
and red-blue-red political corners,
the gladiatorial small screen beings;
they bend their back-stabs front ways in,
claim losers are degrees of winners;
these days the ones who fight to the death
are by law larger than life
and let alone draw blood,
it would be outrageous
if they got in each others hair.
What you have is a variation
on not quite the same dogma
from similar different waxworks,
our monuments of hard-sale Englishness,
or a watered down originality in triplicate;
we hardly choose the fate of our nation
when we nominate the muscle of a media giant
(does anyone know the whereabouts of a David?).

Shadows of *Visionwald*:
Proto Film Script

"The long poem can divide opinion—set reactionary against free thinker, elevate verse as an engine of surprise art, vehicle of coded maverick expression."

Journey to the mind of *Vane Marter*, famed author of *Visionwald* notes

Space closes, tarmac and distance,
sunlight cuts through screen grime,
fan-shaped spectrum on silver disc,
momentum paced near a gearshift,
music over air noise and engine,
a vehicle is tracing easy curves.

Readings arrive in digitals on dash,
numeric consumption, values on dials,
a slipstream skyline, lane, junctions;
Style Driver prone, guiding the wheel,
he recalls research, tutorial sessions,
Visionwald notes revealing *Vane Marter* . . .

112.7 *Visionwald foundation notes studied by Style Driver and Rider 5*

*Vane Marter, some distance from power,
his rule of Risen First starts to weaken;
Lanetta takes over as supreme leader,
a tactician, decorated in recovery wars;
so Vane Marter founds The Golden-Far,
brutality preached to crowded party halls,
a dogma of emblem, mantra and magic,
in stages, building a mania of support,
he recites messages, coded repetitions:
"the unknowns doubt our strength,*

intruders are the disease, lash out at them,
heretics tamed by our finest _Skinnerguns_."

Road movie, dead bikers
in the slipstream of Marter

Rider 5 sits at _Style Driver_'s side;
look of apathy, he blanks his partner;
eyes downward from view ahead,
he concentrates, lowers his voice:
"just intelligence—atypical thinking,
individuals swallowed by a nation,
tempered sadist, shaping the human."

Electronic displays, brake fluid, oil,
bronze oval hangs on the rear view,
a worn out symbol, creed that failed,
bikers stream past, making for town;
their deaths marked on lush verges,
tributes of flowers tied to fencing,
on a road followed by _Vane Marter_.

114.23 revelation notes:
revolt, lessons of defeat

Reasoning, blueprint beginnings,
for notes to edge into versions;
Vane Marter, groomed anarchist,
luminary of the mind evolving;
he can work his malevolence,
a chameleon who absorbs power,
submerges his flow of bloodlust;
Marter will upstage who we are,
guide us with a measured rage.

In place as master of the opportune:
June 14, new semester, <u>Storren</u> rising;
night of rioting . . . procession of voters,
speaker fires pistol into opposing faction,
mass insurrection—guards engage rebels,
arson in the senate rooms, return to order;
lead spokesman identified as <u>Vane Marter</u>,
storming of government, quelled by force,
escape to <u>San Gallay</u>, in disarray, defeat.

Shared miles of groundwork, disciples reveal their doubts

Driver in transition, steady;
his focus copied in rear view,
a reflection forms his portrait,
bone structure, cold expression,
his face pointing at instruments,
he gauges *Rider*, person image,
shaped and fluid, likeness settles;
Rider's short hair, bruised cheek,
even features, tall, muscular thin,

clean jaw-line, his eyes scan;
Driver in sleeveless, assessing,
runs over plan, remains of smile,
bottom lip shields irregular teeth.
Vehicle picks up speed, right fork,
scroll of storefronts, unlit buildings;
Rider slides hand into travel bag,
he pulls out the folded papers,
re-orders sheets, addresses *Driver*:

"Listen *Driver*—this is our brief;
the insurgent they call *Vane Marter* . . .

we have to unearth more *notes*;
it's about nerve, breaking the code,
his spellbinding way with a mob."
Driver pauses, recites under breath . . .
"An orator who intoxicated crowds,
seductive phrases of hatred and fear,
he sourced control, craving the risk."

116.4 notes: mythology
incubates in a voice

2,000 in the <u>Fennermont Hall</u>,
raised fists into haze of smoke,
a sense of union, release from self,
crowd drawn to an honoured soldier,
a tall frame, gloves, military coat,

polished boots on makeshift stage,
a manipulator in awe of himself;
emotive message sent from platform,
he feeds and draws on the mass,
seductive words in guttural drawl:

"go outwards to newfound soil,
disperse those tainting our blood."
His hands slice their movements,
signals, a display of patterns,
belief set in smouldering eyes.

Honour in the school of weapons,
training complex—munitions game

Driver tightens grip on machine gun, levels aim,
tension in face, *Rider* sweeps camcorder on arc,
panning angles of *Driver*, fix of concentration;

they switch over, *Driver* swings lens at *Rider*.
Rider at simulator, fires on tide of automatons,
weapon in full extension, steady balanced arm;
a concert of assaults, score confirming skill.

Aggressors move in passageways,
his hand shudders, jerks to gunfire,
falling marauders stream from haze;
Rider plants feet, hips in adjusted range,
with veiled reverence, *Driver* watches,
laser is locked, an arm whips forward,
slider on gun barrel clacks and reloads.

156.6 notes: hypnosis spell, an orator hones a ferment of passion

His eight month rise to complete power . . .
riots spread at the Salmassa elections,
Vane Marter freed from detention cell,
17,000 rally in Cassellon Square,
military police, arms raised on podium,

wild surety, addressing his parade:
"towards triumph, the weak infect us,
they debase our names — seed themselves
to stain achievements, lessen our fate;
history dares us to renew our race."

Making of the *Visionwald* emblem, key letters hijacked from global corporation

11.05, basement of 6 *Exenfield*,
the two kneel on black linoleum,
measures, location tags, timer,
divided carefully between them;

Rider guides a scalpel round shape,

halves the logo of a fast-food chain,
piecing letters into a new symbol,
twin shapes for next emerging cult;
he centres them on a small table,
their coding radiates in the room.

A line of candles surround the symbol,
they spell its purpose in flickering lights,
in the foreground, a thin digital display,
'*Skinnerguns*' scrolls, red dots repeat line,
rules and vision, work of *Vane Marter*,

Driver focuses, speaks methodically:
"they were amazing, his created police;
Skinnerguns, the wrath of *Skinnerguns*",
he tries to invoke spirit of *Vane Marter*,
repeats the mantras, seeking an essence,

sustained by veneration of *Marter*;
willing *Marter* to appear in a guise,
still tyrannical, a fairer messiah,
humane laws for lowest elements,
less zeal to please his younger tribe.

134.3 notes—removal phase, inventing industrial Galtasse

400,000 men, the <u>Visionwald</u> toll,
<u>Galtasse</u> is likely to exceed this,
the template founded by <u>Marter</u>;
his separation plans, pure ideals,
extractor teams sent to social units,

Senior Grender's clinical orders:
"transport 5,000 under twelves,
relocate to drainshaft complex,
single women to wear blindfolds,
issue disposable protective gowns;

take name cards, land documents,
tabulate all artworks of merit;
healthy males to sodium barracks,
identify sick, enforce blood tests,
points system to save the skilled."

Urban refuge, pilgrimage north

CLUES IN THE REFUSE TRUCK

Side street, walls worn to clay bricks;
Driver and *Rider* take the alleyway,
a rusting skip at building's rear door,
broken boards, shells of grey computers.
The pair pull top layer to the ground,
their pen lasers dart for words of *Marter*;
a fortress *Marter* had made his haven,
his *succession notes* stored in airshaft;
diesel sounds grow to furious, they turn,
truck reverses, metal struts block the sky.

MOVING AGAINST THE MARCH

Downhill, random route into town,
drumming builds from the distance,
relentless march of vicious hundreds,
lead by standard-bearer, green uniform,
legs driven in trained formal steps,

empty eyes of glazed resentment,
maroon flag, sectarian version of *Marter*,
Rider and *Driver* walk against them,
Driver buttons jacket, hides his insignia,
aviator shades mask their judging eyes.

ART GALLERY : NIGHTCLUB AND KISSABLE FREAKS

An urban sculpture, steel locking rings,
"yankie, puppa, delta," — paint on fuselage,
early aircraft stats, fighter plane collage;
blowtorch, monkey face and propeller,
human body with its refuelling tank;
later, *Driver* and *Rider* in nightclub;
giant leans, tongues tiny wheelchair girl,
her drunken smile is lit by the strobe;
outside a blond bends over, guy pumps,
she lolls, her mouth gapes, spits out sick.

IDENTITIES CHANGE AND DISSOLVE,
VOX AND *TONE* : CLONES IN LIFT

Empty hotel lift, enter *Driver* and *Rider*,
mirrored cubicle drops through floors;
Driver's image is flashed onto himself,
Rider in double, both in parallel dimension;
surface cut healed on *Driver*'s right hand,
they warp into waxwork semblances,
doors open, in walk *Vox* and *Tone*,
Manyworld versions of *Driver* and *Rider*;
Tone speaks, "M for breakfast, mezzanine",
they exit, the corridor swallows them whole.

MACHINE GLIDES TO A BREAKDOWN,
CARRIAGEWAY FLAT: CHANGING THE WHEEL

Driver and *Rider* in back of car, eyes
clouded and intense, talk of night's events;
at cruising speed the car shakes, pulls over,
offside front tyre is down, drone of cars,
the cabby swears, bends over torn rubber,
Driver takes jack from boot, sets it up;
winds clockwise, chassis rises off ground.
The engine guns, races on carriageway,
to recover time, steering wheel judders,
on lanes they drove the *notes of Marter*.

141.4 *anticipated notes,*
to a future, unity within time

Evidence of 400 BC Asiatic storytellers,
deeds of Marter in spoken legend.
Examples survive for the future of time;
key tenets taped by satellite workers,
patterned vibration, pulses spell words,
Marter flows through timeframe divides;
humankind impaired and restricted,
a race evolves with diminished function,
Marter frees the higher thinking of man,
notes show how to exceed and ascend,

above physical, moral and mind parameters,
the growth: man, Robotoid, Marter-man;
notes that filter to family and generation,
as one truth system collapses and fades,
notes emerge in the spine of a culture,
seeded in history before his Visionwald,

an actuality saved for <u>Visionwald</u> future;
<u>notes</u> as the model for understanding,
words that enrich the values of <u>Marter</u>,
system to redeem the fragility of man.

Seduced by a hologram:
her factors of attraction

Vodka room, Rider slumps in alcove;
silver lounger, high perspex bar stools,
wall widescreen, girls time their dance;
Rider admires the steps of *Creneth*,
her movements glide into view . . .

beamed in layers—a duplication,
Creneth edges forward, filling screen;
crimson four-inch heels, PVC skirt,
her face slips into a crude smile,
a shaped thigh, airbrush enhanced,

priced up: you pay for each sway,
for this option, select 1 *femininity*.
A performance metered, slim belly,
toe stud, rent her warm projection,
hologram moves to the sung words;

repeated lyric, "die by *Skinnerguns*",
remote controlled, cash the royalties,
selling sensual flirts of virtual self,
lover simulation, grope of a doll.
"*Skinnerguns*" sinks in *Rider*'s mind,

renewed memory, trace of latent fear;
in training, he'd learnt all the chants,
and so much is since forgotten,

erased words that lead to *Marter*,
stories passed of his perfection.

Driver fast processes, almost intuitive;
"your name says it, you're the *Rider*,
Vane Marter would approve your rank,
reserve a place in his military corps;
you have to stay in narrow limits,

you value *notes*, but your mind's flawed."
Rider flinches, glares at exactness of time,
he stabs a fist, punches into *Driver*'s side;
Driver is motionless, neutral and resigned,
takes pain without anger, no retaliation.

Driver in a daze—slumped on seating,
remembers earlier journeys with *Rider*;
he fills with flashbacks of old locations,
linked events, searches for an emblem,
a totem to apply to the cult of *Marter*.

In first sleep, he enters disordered dream,
airport lounge, flights numbered as *notes*,
seven-lane highway, it points to *Marter*;
he wakes as their plane hits the runway,
rail shuttle shoots them to the next city . . .

THE END

CAST

VANE MARTER

> **Rank**: Supreme. Founding member of the *Visionwald* cult. Founder
> and leader of the ruling synod of *Visionwald* — *The Risen First*, which
> he later dissolves to form *The Golden Far* — consisting of nine states-
> men supporting his ideology and work.

> **Uniform and ceremonial dress**: 1.Black *"Suckit"* bondage face mask
> with bright orange disks over eyes, short trunk style mouth piece. 2.
> Black latex one piece body suit with interlocking "L" and "T" emblem
> on chest, taken from the mantra "Love and Torture." 3. Bright orange
> cleric's dog collar to represent mystic status and a bridge between the
> spiritual traditions of the East and West. 4. Calf height bright orange
> lace-up army boots, orange laces.

> **Weapon**: 200cm traditional preacher's wand in brass and painted
> bright orange. Spiked head section with sealed vial for containing
> blessing rain or sulphuric acid, release catch to open sprinkle holes
> for dispersing the liquid in a throwing action.

> **Code name**: *"Our Mentine"* as a version of *"Clementine"*.

STYLE DRIVER

> **Rank**: Sub-Supreme. Armed forces personnel in search of *notes* of
> *Vane Marter*.

> **Uniform and ceremonial dress**: 1. Same as Rank Supreme apart
> from clear eyes pieces in *"Suckit"* mask and black laces on calf high
> boots.

> **Code name**: "Eyeman" from eyes seen through clear lenses in mask.

RIDER 5

> **Rank**: Sub-Supreme. Same as *Style Driver*.

> **Uniform and ceremonial dress**: same as *Style Driver*.

> **Code name**: same as *Style Driver*.

LANETTA

> **Rank**: Supreme. *Marter*'s main rival in his struggle to take control
> of the *Visionwald* cult.

> **Uniform and ceremonial dress**: same as *Marter*.

CRENETH

Rank: Employed Hologram. Her function is to entertain members and followers of *The Golden Far*.

SENIOR GRENDER

Rank: unspecified. Military aid to *Vane Marter* and senior officer of the *Skinnerguns*—elite police force responsible for protecting *Marter* and carrying out selected tactical missions.

A-VOX AND U-TONE

Manyworld clone versions of *Style Driver* and *Rider 5*.

RILLION

Off-screen leader of the motorcycle gang called *The Tallics*.

Uniform: gun-metal grey helmet, grey leathers and grey boots.

FEMME ROBOX

Off-screen leader of the motorcycle gang called *The Radiants*.

Uniform: white helmet, white leathers and white boots.

Basement Plane

A big domestic country;
the ground floor meant food and bed,
while play explained the basement.

Down there in its den of light,
electric and natural meeting at grills;
pears and apples were painted in oils,

a cigarette supply behind the settee;
out in the heat-wave marbles rolled in holes,
then winter permanence, snows reflecting sun.

Grass into Ice

Suddenly winter kicked in hard,
our house shut tight as a sealed box;
snows built up so most of everything
was plastered in white or reflected white,
tree shapes were black blood vessels
against the overkill of amazing white.

We were kids with ice hockey sticks,
messing with discs, our fat rubber pucks;
for once adults came into their own,
hosing water in jets on the field;
grass set firm in a sheet of ice,
to be kids, we cut loose on skates.

Sugar Mountains

Everything in the room was an ornament;
the day's visitor moved its mouth,
pink biscuits were mountains on a plate,

where the furniture had no mental colour,
the chair fatter than the television,
a tiled fireplace where it was bad to go.

Inside, windows leant on immediate world;
outside the universe was spying us.

Waker

I rise on the drag of closing night,
you're the morning's clearest call,
free of cussedness or fallow sleep;
you're dawn beside my dozing streak,
I'm a vulture poor in spiral flight,
a wingspan known for its willing fall;

I'm a sunken sun of dark star clusters,
you're northern lights of genial orange;
I'm the south seas in a reservoir phase,
my month is the diary of many doomsdays,
yours is festival, eve of youth and summer,
I lie till the hours scrape, seconds hinge ...

> *you wake me dream state to wary man,*
> *you stand my spine, kiss the vertical one.*

Cold Dark Matter*

In the littered space of electron gaps,
a privacy where protons lag
or constant of neutron warmth,
where a pre-existence comes to be,
masses mill with a grain of dust
and gravity owns a numberless weight:

> *"I wonder why when I move my lips*
> *there is something there that isn't*
> *to do with atoms of air, kinetic*
> *words or smooth filtration of spit."*

> *"Why is it when I shove my hips*
> *there is something else between the*
> *bones and blood and the groin's*
> *internal neck?"*

> *"I question how I hear the world*
> *when sounds cancel in echo, when*
> *songs are dense in adjoining beats*
> *or the fallacy of noise."*

---

* The hypothetical sub-atomic matter which scientists named to help
substantiate the "Big Bang" theory.

Machinehead and the Vehicle Haven

Vehicles would arrive in friction sectors,
their wheels rotating on track and grid line
to circuits built on highway platforms;
steel models moved on parabolic curves
with pause and surge of tuned combustion.
They were bold slabs of elegant transport,
speed sculptures, frames in last corrosion;
electronic guides would programme routes
to phase and burn of an equinox sun;
the sky would darken with toxins of fuel
till engines stalled on a smoke horizon.

> *Machinehead approved of the energy artifice,*
> *the culture of travellers in ritual jams;*
> *he observed the self-controlled machines,*
> *the advance of racers in full momentum,*
> *repair cabs driven by servile men.*

Spectacle: Ad for the Raider

"Avant-garde poetry is innately intricate, hyper-conceptual and obscure—defeatist thinking of the effete, over-intellectual, pompous poet."

X-RAY

I am what I eat:
soft skin warts,
seasoned fruits of the earth,
stress of each voice ingested;
dust driven from far corners
to a local mouth,
loud retort of words,
crass endings unresolved
and circular food of Christ.

GRAPH

I am what I see:
lean elaborate earth age
forms of the tower,
warm blue electric mist,
sectors called *Credence* and *Derision*,
there is a field of constant birth,
a grid of past evolution,
vertical axis is dream ignited,
horizontal is snow and ash.

SCORE

I am what I hear:
turbine wail and song whir;
it tolls on the underplane,
the belt between picture and sound.
A scream will merge with a mild drone,
envelop radio, sermon and train run;
with no drama, no description,
a line of points will divide and meet,
then a brief echo, cry of fission.

AUTOPSY

Working on the corpse
the android dictates to a machine:
"atomic chain of warship hull,
cell form of ape and unborn child;
anomalies in the early chromosome mix,
sensory trace of anger, skill, capillary action;
electron link to magma, graveyard, ribbon,
frail composite of vows, vacuum, water,
discharge base for parable, humour, radiation."

The Introducers

They referred to science
as the dream of recorded life,
respected ferocity of thought,
the ability to abandon logic;
they inherited traits
of the old condition:
intelligence, morality and valour;

realism was raised
to a strand of consciousness,
a plane on which elders
wandered into future and past.
The individual had lost
utility of sign and word;
communication (the transfer of clues),

was usually enacted in a public place;
in each of three identical phases
a numbered crowd would grow
to encircle a caged beast:
in the ritual sequence
a striker would plunge a knife
in the base of the creature's neck,

gouging wildly with rhythmic twists,
waiting for the myth blood
to fountain and steam,
to harden its pigment
on the barbarous mouth,
till death was a pattern
pulsed at the nearby stars.

Aftermath of a Mountainous Decision that Wasn't Made at a Watershed he Intuited as a Plain

By the time he realised
what he must do,
he had already done
too much of precisely
what he shouldn't.

Throw it Away

"To unearth what we divine as a finite truth;
the poet mines this maelstrom of uncertainty."

It's what you can wake to do
with hoards you lovingly own,
your big answers savoured
and somehow free to let go;
time is not always there as
a neat spread of flagstones
with insights along its way;
what next confidence
can you possibly expect?
A love of art can still survive

the day you haul your stash down
to the nearest corporation dump;
intensively interesting life
is just as tempting to ignore;
details can form into structures,
then cause awareness to sharpen.
Being car-cased is a reverie on its own;
KS02 XBE, small silver Mercedes-Benz,
LN53 VGR, blue metallic Citroen estate,
K787 UDX, jade Vauxhall Astra.

People take to these shells,
pulse gains and regret
from window to windscreen;
don't you just love it
when someone is a suction pad
planting a sincerity on you?
What is it that we put aside
that's there and good to be done?
When anger reaches singular heights
a seeming passive comes to follow.

Gang of Strippers and Chrome Poles,
in brown loafers, struggling pisshead

With lust to a place of massed loud perfumes;
slim things bare privates and tits, sexual density.

> *This man has got to do a walk in a drunk identity;*
> *accidental dance steps, the path his practice room,*
> *whole focus anchors each foot that lands too soon.*

Projections, mirror ball, chart songs and vinyl seats,
flaunt of G-strings, shave scars are close to a crotch,
fingers rub nipples, wheelchair punter sips his scotch;
painted toenails cram in sling-backs, spotlit model meat,
pop chorus fades, then a bronzed rump squats on stage,
put pounds in a pint glass, eye the immigrant hot stuff,
blacks, blondes and Slavics—teen lipstick looker fluff,
their best sleaze tricks have bent, skipped and jumped;
I sanction it all, rise to a craze of making judgements.

Poetry Unzipped: Pep Talk to a Trained Beast

*"An artwork absolves then justifies its own
wildest aberrations and excesses—a self-
regulated autonomous creation."*

Poetry assailant then victim, a gangster of imagined,
cause of huge word acts conjured for platforms or pits ...

*Poetry sees innocent cruel kid test endurance of bugs;
magnifying glass full sun laser beam on beetle shell,
cooking shiny rind, burn hole sweet fume smoke trail,
still hand drills black insect—to work at life's collapse,
ignite pile of dry leaves under car's warming fuel tank.*

Poetry, they scavenge your thing, secretly crave your breath,
you're knowingly lost, a schooled savage, chained and free.
Praise, lash a poisoned claw at street shop volume prose,
shun makers of plays, stalk them, condemn as you bless.
You can do nothing, bypass, defend the worst abandoned;
go on, dare to be the staggering failure some expect to see,
wield a snarling mouth, use the air from unvisited skies.